THE HOLLYWOOD CHRONICLES OF A FEMALE TECH FOUNDER

N.D. ZERMAN

DEEPSTORY PUBLISHING

www.deepstory.ai

www.scriptbook.io

PUBLISHED BY DEEPSTORY

www.deepstory.ai

hello@deepstory.ai

ISBN 9789083667218 (paperback)

ISBN 9789083667201 (hardcover)

ISBN 9789083667232 (eBook)

ISBN 9789083667225 (audiobook)

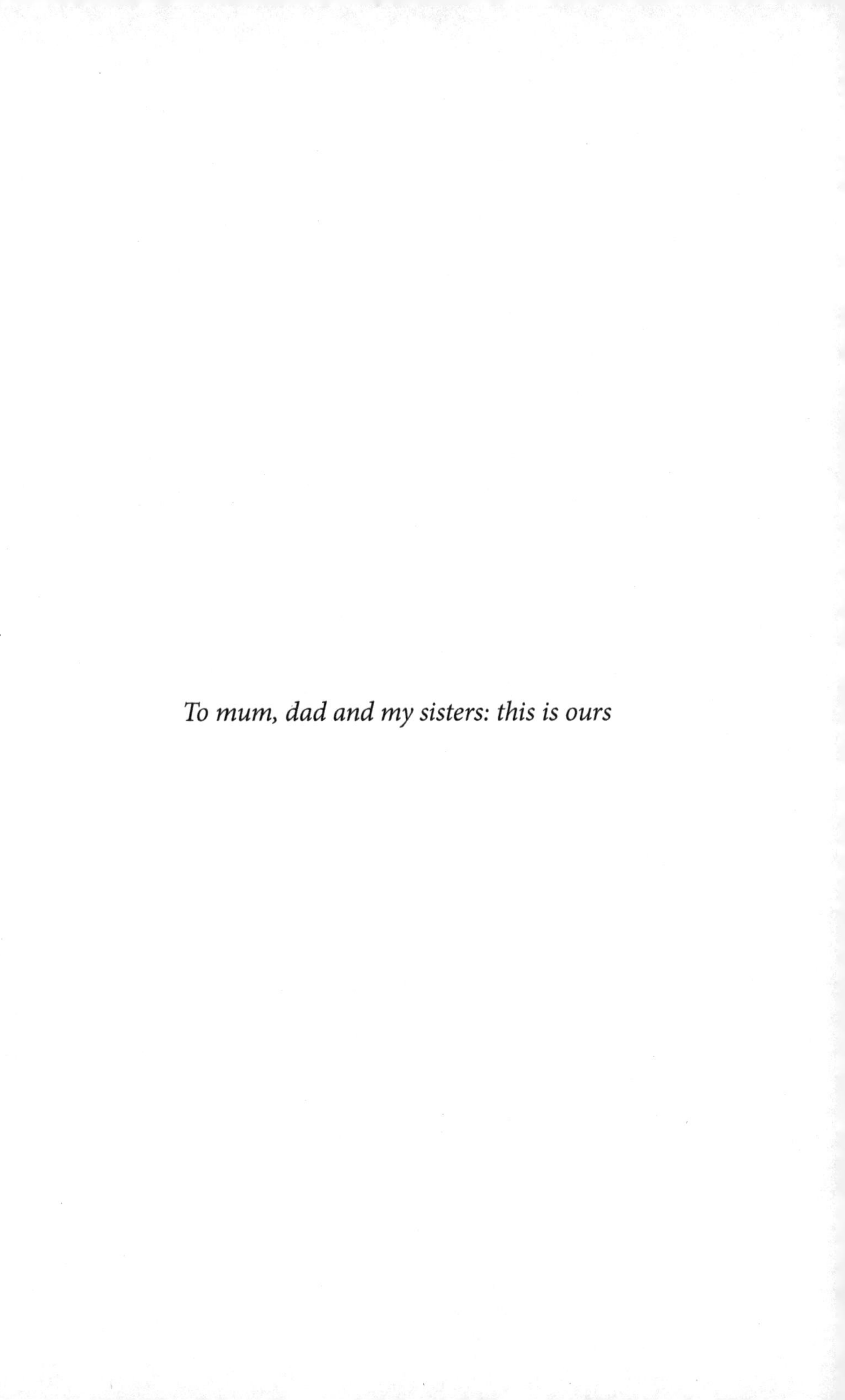

To mum, dad and my sisters: this is ours

CONTENTS

INTRODUCTION

I was twelve years old when my teacher asked us what we wanted to be when we grew up. I wrote, "I want to be a legend." Nothing has changed. Sure, I've got a couple more decades under my belt, a wealth of experience and knowledge that have (*God, I hope they have*) sculpted me into a different person than I was when I was young. But as a child, I sat at my desk in my curly pigtails, in a classroom surrounded by only boys who knew I didn't belong there and wrote that I wanted to be legendary. I knew that one day, people would remember my name.

Here, at my desk with a spiced cocoa in one hand and laptop keys under the other, I'm writing in oversized glasses and a messy bun, curls breaking free in their inimitable chaos. I'm alone in my apartment, but I'm surrounded, even if not physically, by the specters of people who have pushed me into the corner I find myself in tonight. And if you asked what I want to be — who I will become when I grow up? My answer hasn't changed.

I still believe in that little girl's vision of who I am now, in who I can become. I came from immigrants, from parents who worked themselves to the bone to help me rise. I clawed my way into the schools I wanted to attend, whether or not they wanted me, and then into a vocation that wanted nothing more than to push me out. I built something beautiful in a space dominated by the powerful. And then, through a series of happenstances, my own mistakes, the mistakes of others, and more than anything, the circumstance of being who I was in a world of people who wanted to tear me to shreds, that beautiful thing collapsed.

No one is proud to say that they are going bankrupt — that their life's world has fallen like sand through their fingers. But I want to tell the world. I am standing here on these ashes, and I want you to know my story. I want you to see the injustice that runs through the modern landscape of technology, from Silicon Valley to Hollywood, and have you learned from my mistakes in hopes you might build something beautiful of your own. And because of this, I have decided to speak. Strength runs through me like the sugar in this cocoa, and though I'm typing this from, quite honestly, one of the lowest points of my life—well, every legend needs a mountain to climb. This is mine.

HOW IT STARTED

I am, first and foremost, the daughter of immigrants. My parents left Morocco for Belgium in the 1970s, and as you can imagine—as is the case now, quite frankly—, that was not exactly the recipe for accumulating instant riches. My parents have always worked very hard to make a life for themselves and for their children, but ultimately, they came to this country with very little. And no matter which way you slice it, people look on those not from around here differently. That's just the way of it.

Not only were they Moroccan, my parents had five children—four daughters and a son. That's a whole lot of mouths to feed. So, to put it plainly, I grew up poor. I don't know that we *knew* it; you often don't when you're a child. But on some level, it was clear. We didn't get thrown into extracurriculars, and we were never surrounded by mountains of toys. There just wasn't room in the budget for those kinds of things. The money each month was spent before it was earned on rent and food and keeping the lights and heat on.

But if there is one thing kids are going to figure a way to do, it is play. And for me, for my siblings, that meant *to imagine*. I grew up poor on funds but absolutely rich in imagination. Hobbies that cost any amount of money were out, so my siblings and I spent a lot, and I mean a *lot*, of time in the library. We threw ourselves into books. I was that little kid you see in the movies: the small girl with a determined gait, hair in her face, and a sparkle in her eyes, marching right up to the circulation desk with a pile of books taller than she was. Before long, the librarians knew my name. My house was warm and supportive; I wasn't Matilda. Life wasn't something to escape; I didn't need to. Instead, books were a way to lose myself, to play pretend in a different life, a different world, a different set of dreams to chase. But the books I checked out weren't about dragons and magic and babysitters' clubs. I never really felt the need to check my closets for a way into Narnia. The books I thirsted for were biographies — stories of extraordinary people. Not characters who brought magic into the world and let me live in a world of fairies, but people, *real* people, who had made the world I lived in vibrant and real just by walking through it. I didn't want to slay dragons; I wanted to change the world.

At ten years old, I pored over biographies of people like Isaac Newton, Bruce Lee, Nikola Tesla, every name I could find who had had a true impact on the world, especially if those people had battled real hardship to get there. I couldn't stop thinking about Tesla, for instance, the man who had fought everything, given up everything, to change the entire landscape of the earth, change the lives of billions of people who came after him to bring electricity to humanity. Those were the people I stayed up late reading about under my covers with a flashlight after bedtime. I dreamed about discovering something, creating something, not just to sustain myself, but to save the world. When you're a child, you dream big. Hopefully, that never gets taken from you. I sometimes feel that it has been taken from me. But I hope, in my heart of hearts, that it hasn't.

As a child, I always dreamed and hoped and lived big, with passions that burst out of my skin, no matter how tiny and tender that skin might have been. I was granted the gift of reading, the gift of supportive parents, and a mind that knew from the beginning that it craved *answers*. And I was gifted the time and space to allow my brain to wander. To ask. To linger in creativity. I never really played with dolls or aspired to have a Barbie dream house in my bedroom. I didn't fantasize about getting a pony. On the rare occasions on which I got toys, I did crazy things with them. I remember the day my parents finally bought me a bike. This was a big deal! We didn't have money for things like *bikes*, especially not since there were a full five of us to get bikes for. But that day, I got mine, and I was absolutely thrilled—not to ride it but to take it apart.

My parents looked for me outside, expecting to find me wobbling down the street, learning to ride. Instead, they found me in my room with the bike upside down with the wheels popped off it and my little hand around the bike chain. I looked up, hair wild, and hands covered in grease, and I said simply, "I want to know what makes it *go*." They didn't need to worry; I was, of course, going to put it right back together in a second! (I'll spoil this for you now: I did *not* put the bicycle back together as advised by the manufacturer.) That was far from the most disastrous situation my little scientist's spirit ever got me into. It wasn't just experience and taking things apart, see. I also loved to build. One day, my parents asked me what I wanted more than anything in the world, and I sighed wistfully, staring into the middle distance like a Disney princess dreaming that someday her prince will come and answered, "A toolkit." Lo and behold, my parents bought me that toolbox and the overalls to go with it. At ten years old, I was truly living the dream, toddling around my house in my big laborer's overalls, toting my toolbox right along with me. As all ten-year-old girls do, I had a little toy machine that was meant to measure voltage, and it was the day's goal to figure out the voltage on the power outlet in the living room. You know, typical stuff. I marched right over to the power outlet, jammed the black and red probes of my little machine into it, and promptly plunged the entire house into blackout darkness. My parents were thrilled. The point, apart from my clearly having parents who ought to be serious candidates for sainthood, is that this was *always* who I was. This… this wild curiosity and determination and will to understand and test and build and be a part of science and discovery and something great… This was not something I grew into. It is who I am. It is part of my DNA.

Maybe, then, it is not so surprising that my schooling went the way it did. In Belgium at that time, schools were mixed when it came to gender, but only technically. You see, STEM education (Science – Technology – Engineering – Mathematics) was still largely considered boyish; it just wasn't aimed at girls, and girls were generally, if not explicitly, then at the very least implicitly, discouraged from pursuing careers and education in that field. We weren't expressly disallowed from studying technology or engineering, and I certainly wasn't discouraged from interest in such things in my household (evidenced by the overalls and constant bicycle autopsies), but it just wasn't the typical route for girls to travel. Today, there's something of a global push to get girls involved in technology and engineering, but even still, there's a huge gender disparity in these fields, both in careers that focus on these areas and in the education to get them there. Three decades ago, the gap was even more stunning. When it was time for me to leave primary school and go into a higher level at around twelve years old, I was faced with a huge decision: go to the nearby mixed school or go across town to the boys' school. By this point, you can probably already make an educated guess as to where I chose, and you'd probably be right. But let me paint you the full picture in case you're not quite ready to lay money on that hypothesis.

The school nearby would have given me a quality education. Quite honestly, there was nothing wrong with it. It was the school my mother wanted me to attend, and it would have been, by nearly every measure, a good and convenient choice. The school across town was specifically focused on STEM. That area of study was even more male-dominated than it is now, a claim bolstered by the school's student body: one thousand boys… and ten girls.

Though it was literally made up of ninety-nine percent boys, that school was, of course, the one I was determined to attend. It wasn't that I was concerned about being subversive. I didn't pay attention to things like gender stereotyping or bucking tradition at the time; I was twelve years old! I just happened to like overalls and toolboxes, and more than anything, I loved technology. I loved processes. I loved engineering. I loved cutting open the world around me with a scalpel and studying it under a microscope and figuring out the answers to how, exactly, it functioned. It didn't matter to me that receiving an education in those things meant going to a boys' school. Frankly, it didn't occur to me at any point that I shouldn't, that those things were not for me. I loved them, I had a passion for them, so of course they were for me. I told my mother right away— that was the school I wanted to attend. She panicked. "There's no way you're going to that boys' school, Nadira." It wasn't that my mom wanted to limit my opportunities; she never did. My mother encouraged me to be everything I ever wanted to be. It was that she was afraid. There were no girls there; I would be absolutely surrounded by males and subject to all the risks that entailed. There would be no support for me, no infrastructure for my gender (were there girls' bathrooms?), fewer opportunities, and a far greater chance of social ostracization. There were a thousand reasons I shouldn't go. And in reality, she was right about all those things. I knew that what she was saying wasn't foolish; the facts weren't wrong. It's just that I wanted what I wanted badly enough to ignore the reasons not to go.

My mom, on the other hand, wanted to protect her daughter. She went to the mixed school up the road and enrolled me for the upcoming year. So, I spoke to my father. My father was an academic. He and my mother came from two different worlds; she was illiterate, a smart woman who never got the chance to learn to read or write where she grew up. My father, on the other hand, made a career out of education. He lived in academia, so to him, my wishes to study what I wanted made perfect sense. He'd devoted his entire career to that idea and had a deep love of study himself, after all. I came to him crying after my mother registered me elsewhere, begging not to be made to go to the mixed school where I was enrolled. He promptly marched me into the boys' school and enrolled me there.

On the first of September, school was slated to start. I was enrolled in two completely different institutions. I got up, got dressed, and had no idea which doors I would be walking inside. I waited there in my living room, shoes and socks and hair done up, ready to go, not knowing, down to the minute, how the day, the month, the year ahead of me would go. My mother said, "Nadira, you aren't going to that boys' school." In fact, she was so consumed with worry over this possibility that she told me that if I went to the boys' school, I would be punished. My father said, "It's what you want. Just *go*." I was torn apart. On my first day of high school at twelve years old, I was faced with one of the biggest choices of my life. It's rare that a crossroad is laid out in someone's life so starkly.

That something presents itself to you like this, nearly literally like Robert Frost's poem. *Two roads diverged in a wood, and I…*

I've often thought back to that moment, me in my Mary Janes in my childhood living room, my father's car keys in his hand, asking me what life I was going to choose. I've wondered, especially in the midst of all the chaos in which I find myself today, how much about my life would have turned out differently if I had chosen differently that day. If I had listened to reason and logic and the fear of the negative consequences that I absolutely *did* have to face on a daily basis, my life would be drastically different. Or would it? I don't know the answer to that question. But I do know that to have chosen to walk any other path would have been the wrong one. *I took the one less travelled by.* I stood tall and clenched my small fists, jutted my chin out, like I still do when I'm feeling brave, and I said, "Punish me, then. I'm going to the boys' school." *And that has made all the difference.*

BOYS WILL BE BOYS

spent six years in high school; that's how long it lasts in Belgium. And those years were some of the longest in my life. It might seem like my mother was exaggerating in her anxiety for me — that she was being overprotective. Surely, if I was the main character in an animated movie, my mother would have been cast as the antagonist, shamelessly standing in the way of her rebellious daughter's dreams. But in reality, she wasn't. Everything she feared for my schooling life came true. It was as difficult as my mother had said it would be.

As it turned out, it wasn't easy being the only girl in a class of 27 boys who thought they knew everything. And it wasn't just my gender that painted a target on my back. I was also the only first-generation kid in school. The other students made it very clear that they didn't think I belonged here. What was I doing, coming into a Catholic school like this, one meant for *boys*—everyone knew that! — and acting as though it was my right to be here? Then there was the issue of my race — and their racism. I had the nerve to be a Moroccan, a Muslim, and an immigrant. Hearing "go back to your country" was a daily thing for me. I endured the worst type of racism and sexism during those six years. Never mind that the school *was* legally mixed. Never mind that I was born in Belgium

— not that such a thing ought to matter. Never mind that I had the same right to sit in that classroom as any of the Belgian boys there. I was bullied for it, and that bullying was relentless. It was maybe worse because it wasn't just the other students who made it clear what they thought of my presence there. It was the teachers, too.

Whether explicitly through asking me flat out what my goals were there, or implicitly, those teachers looked down their noses with expressions that said, "*What is she doing here? Why am I wasting my time answering this little Moroccan girl's questions? This isn't a field of study for her. It's a school for future engineers. And we all know she isn't going to be one.*" There was no place for a Moroccan girl in the world they'd created. Since they had no place in their world for me, I carved one for myself. That was something I was always good at.

I was the first Moroccan girl to attend that school, and whether I had the right to be there wasn't something that so much as crossed my mind. Then, that same year, I apparently decided that being the first to go to a Catholic boys' STEM school wasn't quite enough of a challenge to give myself. I decided that what I really wanted was to learn a martial art. My parents clearly hadn't learned from giving me the bike and the toolset, or maybe they had. I can hear the discussion now: *Oh God, what could she do with the power to kill with her bare hands?* After asking multiple times whether a martial arts class might be able to find its way into the budget, my parents acquiesced. I imagine it had a lot to do with the fact that, despite my mother's adamant protests, I truly *was* surrounded by nothing but boys, and learning how to defend myself would, in all likelihood, prove useful. It did.

I was bullied and harassed every single day of my high school career. And I don't mean that mean things were said to me. They were, of course, but that wasn't the extent of it. The boys in my school made fun of me, but they also bullied me physically. They shoved me, tried to trip me in the halls, pulled my hair. We see it everywhere in wildlife shows, right? The Jackals work together to pick off the weak one in the pack. But I wasn't weak. They quickly learned that if they hit me, I would hit back. I was five-foot-three and weighed ninety pounds, but I threw a *lot* of punches in high school. And I was good at it. I was the first girl to ever come to that karate school, and the first Moroccan girl, beyond that. By the time I was twelve, I was already building the life story of a true pioneer. A history of *being the first*. Eventually, I would come to wonder if that part of me would ever be satisfied and sit back. If I would ever get to experience activities and groups and aspirations that included just getting to be a part of something without having to be the *first*. I don't think I will. I don't know that I really *want* to anymore.

Perhaps, some part of me does, I can admit. On my saddest days, when I look around and recognize the things that are falling apart around me, when I really analyze all the things you lose when you have to be the first to do something, some small piece of me that I try not to interact with much whispers that my days of trailblazing should end. Or that if only they *were* over, things could be so easy. And don't I want that? But the truth of the matter is that I don't. And I didn't want it then. I didn't need it. Being the first is hard. Blazing a trail is a cliché, but if you think on this, what it means is that you are the one starting the fire that cuts the path. You're the one inhaling the smoke, chopping down branches with a machete and getting hit in the face with the thorns again and again when the trail doesn't go the way you planned. But it means that you also get to be the one who isn't hemmed in by limits. You get to see things no one ever dreamed. If you are condemned to a life of being the first, you may show up with smoke stains and scars on your face, but at least the world is *never* a cage. You always see from the panoramic view from the seat. It is a sometimes hard, sometimes unimaginably painful, expanse of possibility. It certainly felt that way when I was a child.

I threw myself into karate, like I did (and still do) into everything I cared about. When I let myself go from taking martial arts to really *becoming a martial artist*, I excelled. After taking karate for a decade, I earned my black belt. My parents' house is filled with medal after medal and ribbon after ribbon, because I won nearly every kumite tournament I ever entered and became regional champion several times. I may have been small, but I was a natural at kicking ass. The boys at school learned that the hard way. The more my confidence and skills in combat grew, the harder it was to pick on me. A boy would trip me, and I would throw a punch. He would pull my hair, and I would throw another. I spent an entire high school career with hyperawareness of my surroundings and flying hands and feet. I had no qualms about throwing high kicks and hard hits and wasn't shy about kicking boys right in the nuts.

Boys who are taught that they own the world aren't often particularly good at listening to girls. But when their testicles are involved, suddenly their hearing improves. Slowly, I developed a reputation as someone not to be messed with. My willingness (that sometimes bordered on eagerness) to fight in the hallways came with a constant barrage of newspaper articles about my tournaments. Results, month after month, were printed in the papers and talked about everywhere, as high school sports results generally are, and it gave me the smallest bit of relief in the halls. Eventually, it became clear that I wasn't going to be easy prey. The set of my jaw told them not to mess with me, and my busted knuckles backed it up. That didn't mean they stopped. I don't think

I ever faced a year of high school in which I was *truly* left alone. But the bullying slowed. I was able to survive.

To this day, I am so immensely grateful to my parents for allowing me, even in the midst of such a difficult challenge as conquering a boys' STEM school in the late nineties, to take on yet another that seemed so daunting. While I was getting taunted and bullied every day, karate gave me something to excel at. It gave me a reason to believe in myself — to keep pushing. It gave me strength and courage and the self-esteem that my classmates and so many of my teachers seemed to be really trying their best to chip down to nothing, piece by piece. Honestly, I try not to think about high school much.

I suspect I'm not the only one who has that feeling about the time. Only a few of us are really graced with a beautiful high school experience, the kind we can look back at fondly as our best days. I was not one of them, and I bet that most of the people reading this weren't either. It was a time filled with confrontations with assholes. High school was (and is) uniquely tough. It's not a time period I reminisce about in pastel shades and dulcet tones. For me, I suppose it's that I resent what they stole from me. I went into this school determined enough to face punishment, to really soldier on against the odds for something I loved. Something that seemed as impossible to give up as breathing. I'm angry, looking back, that it took six years for those boys, those teachers, to rob me of the greatest loves I've ever known—my love for technology.

By the time I was seventeen, engineering and technology were no longer the reasons my heart beat — the reasons I got up in the morning. I hadn't forced my family home into darkness for the sake of exploration in a long time (remember the probes in the socket that blew all the fuses when I was a kid?). There were no pieces of things taken apart, no screws on the floor, no oil on my hands. They took that from me, and I don't know that I'll ever get rid off the leftover hollow in my heart. But I graduated. I finished. I can tell you that I did what I came to that school to do. And at the end of six years, I walked across that stage, got my diploma, and I never looked back. Onward to the next discovery.

NEW YORK, NEW YORK

High school was a nightmare. But university was a completely different story. I entered university that fall with renewed hope in my heart and a spring in my step. High school was over, and I was an adult. I was going to be an engineer. Finally, after years of struggle, this was it. I was, once again, a minority — being a woman in any kind of STEM field comes with that. There are just generally far fewer women in these fields for any number of reasons. But I wasn't *alone*. I wasn't a target. I didn't have to spend nearly all my mental reserves on grit and self-defense; I could devote them to learning. My first semester at university was a revelation. I'd been working so hard for this — for what felt like my entire young life, and finally, I had it.

Then, eight months into my course of study in a university I loved, in the field I'd dreamed about, I got news that shattered my world: my brother had died. The news was devastating. I don't know that anything I've ever experienced has so thoroughly knocked the wind from my lungs. My brother was the only one I had, and he was the eldest. He was, in a word, my hero. I was his little sister; so, of course, I idolized him. Unfortunately, he'd never picked friends particularly well; my parents were always worried about it. And I believe it was ultimately the friends he'd thrown in with that led to his getting killed. It was horrible and tragic, and something you don't ever quite get over. It certainly wasn't something I could study through. I was mired in my grief for the sudden loss of someone who mattered so much in my life, and my parents. Losing a child is something most parents never imagine. It's not nature's order. Parents aren't supposed to bury their children. Ultimately, I decided to leave university just eight months after I'd started. No matter what kind of value I was getting from it, it didn't make sense to stay with my life falling to pieces around me, when I felt that I might come apart at the seams at any moment. So, I packed up and went home.

My parents were inconsolable. My mother was nearly out of her mind with grief, and my father wasn't faring any better. None of my sisters were handling it well, and neither was I. How could we? How does a person, any person, handle a loss like that *well*? I don't think there's a blueprint for what that would even look like. There is no *well*, in situations like this. There is no *handling it*. There is simply experiencing it. And that is what we did. We experienced.

I moved back in with my parents to take care of them; that was the role I took upon myself. You choose roles when something like this happens. The biggest one I felt I needed to play was that of the clown. When you see your parents crying, or trying their damnedest not to, every minute of every day, you'll do anything to make them smile. So nearly all my waking energy went toward that. I was goofy and fun and silly and exaggerated; I was playing a part. And every time one of my parents would crack a rare and nearly impossible smile, it became worth it. Of course, I was exhausted playing my role of the jester. And you know the way it goes with comics and clowns: they're always sad behind those painted smiles. I experienced my grief privately, after hours. When I could take the mask off and be with myself and my sadness, away from the performances I gave in a world that was permanently altered, I would let myself break. I *experienced* my brother's death alone, in my bedroom, while the rest of the house either slept or pretended to.

It took a year before we could all truly begin to experience the new normal together, but eventually we could. Eventually, the days started to look like life. After that year had passed, I could feel it scratching at my skin. Something just beneath the surface, begging to burst free. I realized one day, after staring at the same walls week after week and hour after hour, that I'd never gone beyond here. I'd never so much as left my hometown. A person has funny realizations in the midst of grief, but maybe this one wasn't so odd. It is normal, I guess, for an eighteen-year-old girl to want to fly so badly she can taste it, even if that want comes to her almost overnight. My mother, once again, was nervous. Particularly on the heels of her son's death, she worried about my desire to go overseas. They killed people in America, didn't I realize that? But once again, my father talked her down. I needed to experience my own life, he said. To take the risks I felt burning in my blood. And this was one of those risks.

So, after a few months, I found myself stepping off a plane in the JFK International airport, and breathing in the humid, smoggy freedom of New York City. My mother asked me, before I went, *why* I wanted to go to New York. I think I plagued my mother, filling her mind and mouth with questions of why when it came to my decisions, and I probably still do. The things I want to do are always big, and those kinds of things always come with *why* in some way or another. The answer was simple: I wanted to learn English. We'd had one hour a week of English in high school, just enough to know that none of us knew anything. My English wasn't good, but I felt that the language was the one I would need most when the future came.

So, I got on a plane. And then it landed, and I stepped out of that airport into the city I'd dreamed of for years — a city that still holds a truly special place in my heart. It was the first trip I ever took on my own, and I spent a year as a foreigner learning English in a city that never slept. It was harrowing, it was adventurous, it was breathless. I experienced New York City the way I experienced everything else: all in. I ate the street food (and got sick from the street food), I went to the coffee shops, I struggled to pay rent, and I talked to the people. So much, in fact, that when I came back to Belgium, I came back speaking English with a thick New York accent. Maybe I'd accomplished my goal just a little too thoroughly. But I'd done it.

Even now, writing this, I can't help but smile—the kind of smile that lets me feel my eyes crinkle at the corners. The love I have for that city, for what it is and what it stands for, for what it gave to me—that will forever run in my bloodstream. While I'll always love New York… Los Angeles was a different story. Maybe I should have known, even then, that the ultimate path I chose to pursue with my startup company, ScriptBook AI, was not the path my life was ultimately meant to follow. Maybe I should have had some idea that I ought to go to Los Angeles while I was in America to get the lay of the very strange land. If New York is the heartbeat of America, then Los Angeles is the pulsing center of its neurological system, its brain stem. Or vice versa. The point is, they're both integral to the American identity and spirit, so if I was going to come here, I needed to experience both. So, I bought another plane ticket to complete the set.

I landed in LAX, and it felt nothing like touching down in New York City. New York City felt authentic, real, full of possibility.

The air was electricity and it buzzed and zapped on my skin every second. From the moment my feet touched the dirt there, Los Angeles felt like a place I wanted to leave. The air was dull and dense. I felt weighted to the core. With at least one asshole per capita, it reminded me of my high school days. I could only hope my experience would be sans bullying. I would soon learn that hope was unfounded as I was almost immediately served up a dish of harassment. I worked as a receptionist for a while, in a place that, in addition to the meager pay, offered me free boarding, so surviving there wasn't too much of a problem. But thriving there would turn out to be a mammoth challenge.

Where New York City felt to me like the realest pieces of a dream, the parts you wake up with the memory of, that change the way you walk through the next day, Los Angeles felt like all the false parts. It felt like a plastic city, all airbrushed skin, surgically altered faces, and overly polished smiles. I know that there were dreamers in L.A. and wonderful people who call the city home. It's just that in my time there, Los Angeles never spoke to me; I could never feel its pulse like I could in a hundred other places. And in some ways, I think it's because I sensed falsehood from the beginning. I'm not a person who gets starstruck. I'm not someone who is easily impressed by other people. I *care* about other people, but it is because I see them as fellow humans, not rungs on a ladder or some kind of elevated beings who have risen above me. My mother always taught me that when it comes down to it, everyone breathes. These people in L.A. were people just like myself — people who drool when they sleep, pick their noses, and have to take a dump. That's it. That's the meaning of life, the barest truth there is. You'll walk away from my story with a sparkle in your eye, book clutched to your chest, and tell your book club with a sigh, "Everyone breathes and takes a dump!"

Maybe that was why I was never enchanted by the magic of Los Angeles with its perfectly sculpted bodies, perfectly coifed hair, and perfectly straight teeth. The sparkle never quite made its way into my heart. So, I left L.A. for Belgium again, not intending to make it many years later the home base of my startup company ScriptBook AI. I thought I'd seen the last of it. I was wrong. My experience with L.A. can be summed up in this: one day, I looked out my window to see that the streets below me had been closed down. They'd been closed because they were filming *Gigli*. Now that was *cool.* I got to see a film set, and for the first time there, I was truly dazzled. But *Gigli* did about as much for Bennifer (Ben Affleck and Jennifer Lopez) as Los Angeles did for me. My dark prophecy, my predictive omen, came in the form of a film with a six percent rating on Rotten Tomatoes.

GIGLI

Back in Belgium, I found that my spirit was rejuvenated. After spending so much time sleepwalking through grief, it was like my time in the United States had kicked me back into living. I re-enrolled in university, this time in a field far removed from the difficulties and passions of my childhood and very young adulthood: applied economics. It was a field that involved measures and processes and research but, for me, didn't hold the tainted backdrop that technology and engineering did.

I was successful in my studies, even though it wasn't my first love. It was something to do, something I could do well in, something that would give me security and a career to lean on. I worked and studied hard, and in my final year of university, the time came for my master's dissertation. I was most interested in predictive modeling, a way to take economic theory and use it for something tangible. I pored through research and potential topics. While economists are portrayed like James Bond in films, dodging explosions, getting the girl, and smoking Cuban cigars afterward, shockingly… economics can be really, *really* dull.

One night in the library, as one only tends to do when one is researching something really, *really* dull, I found myself thinking about the movie *Gigli*. *Gigli*, as mentioned earlier, was one of the biggest flops of the decade. It wasn't just a film that quietly came into and then left our collective consciousness in a dignified whisper. *Gigli* belly-flopped, and it did so spectacularly—with a slap that could be heard echoing across the entire film industry. There were newspaper articles and segments about it with people from all over the industry (and some outside it!) analyzing it to death. This was a film with two A-listers—and A-listers who were great at courting publicity. It had a good budget, distribution, everything. By all measures, it should have succeeded. But, in the greatest understatement of the century: it didn't. In that quiet library, under the hum of the fluorescent lights and the warmth of the surrounding textbooks and ceiling-high shelves, I chewed the end of my pencil and thought about *Gigli*. Perhaps, I realized, for all my complaints about Los Angeles, there was something about my time in that place that I could take and use to my advantage. Yes. I had an idea. I presented the idea to my professor: I wanted to research film projections. To use predictive modeling to make educated and accurate assumptions about which films might succeed at the box office and which might fail, catastrophically or otherwise. Surely there was some gem to be found if a person dug deeply enough into this.

I may be the first on the planet to have ever said this sentence, but really, it all came back to *Gigli*. *Gigli*, my friends, was where it all began. Somewhere in the distance, a crow caws, signaling a dark and terrible future. I ignore the signposts. I'm a pioneer, remember? That's what we do. We start off on adventures inspired by *Gigli* and come back with one eye missing, tales of a close run-in with Medusa, and all our money lost on the conquest.

My professor approved my research project, and I was off. To my pleasant surprise, there was tons of data on predicting box office performance of movies, enough to devote myself to its study for a year. My biggest resources were Wharton, MIT, and Harvard, whose research groups had clearly dedicated to an enormous amount of research to this topic. The film industry, you see, is immensely unsuccessful. Hollywood is nothing if not gilded. It is covered in gold paint so it shines, but the second you scratch, the gold flakes off and crumbles. Studies have shown that fewer than twenty percent of films that are produced make money at the box office. That's right: a full eighty percent lose money. When you hear about these movies making hundreds of millions of dollars, remember that those are outliers! They are not the rule; they are the exception. Eighty-six percent of films never so much as recover their costs.

This is such an issue in an area of the world that is known for funneling money through itself like it's nothing, that there has been a huge amount of research dedicated to fixing it. In the right climate, if someone could figure out how to fix this problem, they ought to be able to walk out with an absolute boatload of cash. That wasn't my intention at first; I was a college student. My intention was to get a passing grade. I did. I compiled data set after data set and applied economic theory and the concept of predictive modeling to an industry that essentially functions like the wild west with a strong dash of nepotism thrown in, and what I came out with on the other side was something beautiful. I was truly proud of my work. It was such a good dissertation, in fact, that my professor suggested that I take what I had and begin work on a Ph.D.

Because I am, for better or for worse, hopeful and unmistakable, I said, "Yes! That's it! A Ph.D. is for me!" I was going to change Hollywood. But had I watched my sister struggle her way through her doctorate program, I might not have been so enthusiastic. She's absolutely brilliant, and she succeeded—her degree of study was in the medical realm— but she would come home every day, burned out and miserable. She said, "Nadira, don't do this. Look at me. If you dive into this world, you'll be haggard and sobbing daily. Don't do it unless you *need* to." From this vantage point, academia suddenly looked a lot like hell. The longer I thought about it, the more I came to realize that I was sick of studying. My heart was no longer in school. I'd achieved a lot in a little time, and I'd gotten my degree. It was time to move on to greener pastures. So, in the end, I took my sister's advice. I graduated, and I took my degree and my research with me. I found a job, one that had honestly very little to do with my degree (as a rite of passage), and I put my dissertation in a drawer. It had been a grueling year, and the idea of turning around an industry with my ideas had been exciting! But the timing wasn't right. It was a beautiful dream I would have to place in the freezer for a time. I prayed it didn't get freezer burn!

Then came the year 2014. After a long wait, the day finally arrived to thaw out my dissertation and present it to the world — the world of film, that is. An accelerator came to Belgium looking for tech startups to jumpstart. These kinds of accelerators were very popular all over Silicon Valley — programs with a whole lot of money to burn, looking to spend it on the hottest young innovators. They want to get in on the ground floor of thrilling new technology, and the way to do that is through mentorship, workshops, and venture capital. And one of these Accelerator programs came to Belgium.

This was it; this, I decided, was my time. This was the moment I would jump into the industry and see if I could turn my idea into something truly workable. I pulled my thesis out of the drawer it had come to call home, quietly waiting for a reason to come alive. I dusted it off and repackaged it to send to the Accelerator program. I basically grabbed chunks of my thesis, drew from all that research and that year of work, and I used it to explain what I wanted to do and, more importantly, why it would succeed. There were over 850 applicants to the Accelerator program — applicants far deeper into the process than I was, all with co-founders, nearly all men. And there I was, a woman with an idea. Alone. The odds seemed truly impossible, because they were. But then, the unimaginable happened. It was announced that, of the 850 startups that had applied to the Accelerator program, ten were selected. Those selected applicants would be incorporated and given $25,000 of startup money, coupled with direction and mentorship to truly start something they'd dreamed of. And I was one of them!

As was the pattern of my life until now, it was me alone in a group of men. The nine other startups, all male, were made up of co-founders, then there was me, standing alone. I was quickly informed by the managing partner of the accelerator that I was required to choose co-founders. In fact, if I *didn't* find someone to share responsibility with, even though the idea was mine, I would be kicked out of the program. What I truly wanted was a team, not co-founders. I wanted to take my idea as far as it could go, to spearhead something great that I had created on my own. I wanted a group of innovators around me who could help me achieve what I wanted for the company that had slowly begun to form in my head, and I wanted to do it as the head of that company. But I also wanted that $25,000. So, at this program's insistence, I located co-founders. This would turn out to be one of the most massive headaches of my entire professional life.

CO-FOUNDERS DRAMA

Me, a woman in a sea of men in tech, saw twenty-five grand being dangled in front of me. *All you need to do to get it*, I was ultimately told, *is to share.* I reached back into the lessons I'd learned in pre-school, and I decided to play nice. The organization had given me several recommendations, and I approached them with my pitch. Ultimately, I wanted no co-founders, but I found three.

One was a data scientist and two were software developers. It was an easy entry for them. I'd been selected already, the idea was there, and there was $25,000 in startup capital waiting for us. All they had to do was show up. It was child's play. A painful, but important lesson: if you're brought to the crossroads to make a deal, assume the man you're dealing with is the devil. It was clear from the beginning that the aim of these three men was to find a way to push me out, raise more capital, and build my company in their image. That was not a game I was willing to play. From day one, every negotiation was a nightmare. I had my co-founders, but they weren't prepared to play by the rules they'd agreed to begin with. I'd offered a fifteen percent stake for each of them in my company when I invited them on board. After all, it was my research, my work, my idea. They would contribute in some way,

I was sure. But the company was mine. This was easy to agree to at first. But the second the ink was dry; it became another matter entirely. Suddenly, the fifteen percent that had seemed enticing before sounded meager to their greedy ears. The percentage I was offering was right in line with the percentages offered by the other founders; I'd asked around before I made the offers. But it just wasn't enough. My co-founders banded together in their frustration and labeled me a dictator. A dictator, after all, wants power. A dictator wants the majority share, just like I did. I was a terrible person, even though I was honoring the agreement we'd made from the start.

I started flashing back to high school, to all the boys who had tripped me every day and pulled my hair in the hallway. But this time, I couldn't resolve the issue with an uppercut and a swift kick to the nuts. But it was tempting! I did everything I could. I fought back; I held my ground; I went to the people behind the Accelerator program. I couldn't incorporate with men like this, I told them. I could not possibly start a company with men who were actively bullying me like this. I was asked to resolve it, again and again. Eventually the stress got so intense that it began to affect my health. I could barely eat, could hardly sleep. It started to show up on my skin in the form of massive breakouts so painful and noticeable, other people got past their social awkwardness enough to point out the pimple on my cheek that was worthy of the Guinness Book of World Records and ask about it. They were concerned! And they were right to be. *I* was concerned. What the hell had I gotten myself into?

I remember blinking at myself in the mirror one day, hair falling out in damp ringlets around my blotchy face, bags under my eyes big enough to carry a week's worth of groceries. I was looking like a thoroughbred that had been ridden hard and put away wet.

It was time for a serious sit-down with myself. I asked *Mirror Me* if this was what *we* wanted. If this was what *we* had worked so hard for all these years. Was this what startup life was really like? If it was, I wanted no part of it. Then I asked, if nothing changed, could I like this forever. Was it worth it? Even if we made a billion dollars, was I willing to sacrifice all I would lose to get it?

Before the incorporation, it was mandatory that we meet with a counselor who would check on us to make sure we were thriving in this stressful program, or at the very least, surviving it. I wasn't sure I was doing either. This lovely woman sat me down and asked how I was doing. How was the workload? How was I managing my stress? How were things going with my co-founders? I bawled my eyes out. I poured out all my stress onto her shoulders. I told her about my mind and my heart and everything I was feeling. That these men hated me, that they bullied me on a daily basis. That I couldn't sleep, that I couldn't stop thinking about it. That I had no idea what I was going to do. To this day, I am so immensely grateful to that therapist. She didn't tell me I was being too emotional. She didn't tell me that this was normal, that this was something I just had to deal with if I ever wanted to make it in this field. She cocked her head and said, "Nadira, are you sure you want to form a company with *those* men?" The relief that washed over me, at the power in a single question, was palpable. She said, "You can't let them do this to you. You need to listen to your inner voice. You are a strong woman, and this is yours. You can't let them take what's yours and treat you this way. You need to break completely from them and move on. Because let me tell you this: you will acquire other co-founders. Period. You do not. Need. These men."

That woman gave me some of the best advice I have ever received. And more than that, she gave me validation. She gave me agency. She gave me power. I marched out of her office and right into the Accelerator's headquarters, and said to its board, "This is it. I won't incorporate with these men. I'll find someone new if I have to, but there's no way I am putting my idea and my future into the hands of men who bully me. They're out."

The board could not possibly have been shocked, not after the number of times I'd been to their office over the last few weeks. But they were immediately thrust into chaos. "Nadira," they told me, "We *just* finished announcing the program and the selections to the press. We just told *everyone* that we've got a woman, a minority woman, running a tech startup that builds Hollywood software—you're a big story, and we've already told it!" I could feel the panic emanating off them land on my skin. I had the power. They were right where I needed them. Maybe under the weight of all of this pressure, they would finally agree to let me do this on my own. Maybe this was the push they needed. I could—

"You have to find other co-founders," they said to me. And there was the gavel. The judgment was made. Of course, I did. "We don't care if it's those three. If it isn't working out, fine. But you've got to find other co-founders; that's the deal." So once again, I found myself pushed into the process of selecting co-founders. I had never heard the word "co-founder" so many times in my life, and I was beginning to get absolutely sick of it. Some people have visceral reactions to the word "moist." You say it, and they shudder and kick you out of their living room. That's me with "co-founder." Say it in my presence and it's "GET OUT OF MY HOUSE!"

But I found them. One was obtaining his PhD in Artificial Intelligence, and the other was a data scientist. I spoke with them, I listened to my inner voice as much as a high-pressure situation would allow, and honestly? They seemed nice. They didn't give me the impression the others had. I discussed the percentage split with them up front, just as I had the others, and they agreed. This seemed fair and reasonable. So that was it. In a whirlwind, I'd found business partners, and we incorporated. It took less than four weeks for the cracks in the foundation to begin showing.

A few weeks after we incorporated, one of my co-founders stopped showing up for work. Two of us would be in the lab working, and he wouldn't even bother to saunter in late and hung over. What I wouldn't have *given* for him to have shown up late and hung over! He just… didn't come in at all. After tolerating this for a while, I called. "Hey," I said, "So what's going on here? We're all busy, I get it. But I do need you to come in. We've got work to do here to get this company off the ground." My partner and I were diligently working, collecting data, developing technology. And we needed him to do the same. His personal life, he claimed, was a little overloaded at the time. *Fine*, I figured. Not a problem. If he didn't have the time, he could leave. He hadn't done a week's worth of work, which should have made this very simple. He could re-assign his shares to me, head out, and we'd call it a day. No harm done. But that wasn't going to work for him.

I figured that a situation like this would be cut and dry; we could even part on good terms. Frankly, the fewer partners I had in this, the better. But then I received a letter from his lawyer: if I wanted this man to leave my company, it read, I owed him seven thousand dollars. The man had done nothing but sign his name a few weeks prior, but that didn't matter. I privately seethed, allowed myself fifteen minutes of despair. I pondered the situation. And however unjust it felt, it was what it was. I paid him seven thousand dollars out of my precious seed money, and I washed my hands of it. Finally, the real work could begin.

JOE GAZILLIONAIRE

After what felt like an eternity, we were rolling up our sleeves for the dive into developing our product. We'd wasted enough time fighting with co-founders and lawyers, and at this pace, we would never get anything done in time. So, the work began in full force. Once again, I began receiving pushback. My co-founder started complaining regularly, and the chief complaint was always the same: he didn't have enough shares. The fifteen percent he'd agreed to at the beginning of the deal was far too low a percentage; he wanted thirty. The work he was doing was simply too much for fifteen percent of the company to be his reward. I wasn't against raising his stake in the company. In fact, I was open to it. I asked him to come back to me in six months when he'd truly done some software development work, when he had something to show me, and I would absolutely be willing to talk about doubling his stake from fifteen to thirty percent. But no, he wanted to get paid now, needed to get paid now. Unfortunately, it isn't that simple.

The $25,000 we'd received in startup money was necessary, not for personnel, but for server costs, incorporation, legal fees, materials; because of the way a startup company functions, you might walk away from a deal like this making zero dollars a month to begin with. This man wanted five grand a month. We weren't an operating company yet! We weren't rolling, making any kind of product. We were developing who we were in hopes of one day *becoming* a company that could generate a real living for us. I would have absolutely loved to have been able to give him five thousand dollars a month. I would have loved to have given *myself* five thousand dollars a month. But that isn't reality, not with a startup. That isn't the immediate lifestyle you sign up for when you decide to take a gamble on this line of work.

We went round after round after round, and five months into development, I started shopping for venture capital. The weight of raising this capital was entirely on my shoulders, and my co-founder spent the majority of that time complaining. I spoke to two venture capital firms — one private and one public. Both were immensely interested. But they didn't want him; they wanted *me*. I'll be the first to admit: it was intoxicating. I was told that they wanted to invest in my idea, in my company, in *me*.

For the first time in my life, powerful men stood before me telling me that they believed in me, and they had the power to do something about it. It was one of the most exhilarating things I'd ever felt. I was able to raise, on my own, a seed round of 1.2 million dollars—on the condition that my co-founder leave the company. But more good news was just around the corner. My story broke in the Belgian press as the first female founder of a tech startup to raise over a million dollars in venture capital. My legacy of being "first" and "only" continued, even though I didn't want it to. I told my co-founder the news: I had over a million dollars at my disposal, but they wanted him out. And that, ultimately, I agreed. I thought that the best thing for both of us was that we go our separate ways. He agreed to the deal and walked away with ninety grand from the venture capital firms. They took his shares in exchange, and I was finally where I wanted to be: standing on my own two feet, in charge of my *own* ideas and my own company, with the money to do exactly what I needed to succeed.

The investors I secured made a huge difference in my story. My first investor, we'll call him Joe Gazillionaire was a massive deal; he was and remains, one of the biggest investors in all of Europe. His name is well-known enough that no one could believe I hadn't heard of him until I started doing the work to raise this capital. When I finally did, I was told again and again that this was the man to go to, but that it was highly unlikely I'd get so much as a meeting. Joe was enormously important in the venture capital world, and well-acquainted with making waves—he regularly made deals with the biggest names in the world to the tune of hundreds of millions of dollars. He didn't have time to talk to an unknown with nothing but an idea in her hands. To make things more complicated, even if I *could* manage to get a hold of him, Joe's investment firm never invested in startups as the sole money source. To get him to invest, I had to secure a co-investor with whom he would partner. Fortunately for me, I had several contacts at Dray M, a European government-owned multi-billion-dollar investment fund that invests in tech companies.

As you can probably figure by now, I have never been averse to shooting for the stars. I was in a rough situation at the time, seven grand in the hole from the co-founder who had left, and with another co-founder who spent his time sitting on his hands and doing nothing while he waited for his $90,000 paycheck. I had what barely qualified as a minimum viable product. Calling my chances a long shot is to put too high a value on the slim odds. I'd been advised by multiple people not to even try at this point. I had so little to offer; what I needed to do was to develop a prototype, at least. To have something in my hands to show to potential investors, to gain a little traction with customers. By now, you won't be surprised to learn that I decided, instead, to go with my intuition. My intuition told me to hop onto LinkedIn, e-mail one of the most powerful men in Europe and ask if he would be interested in investing in me. So, I did. I shot an email to Joe Gazillionaire, introduced myself, and asked if I might be offering something he was looking for. He was interested. I sent Joe my pitch deck, and he *remained* interested. The fact that I was speaking to Dray M, the European multi-billion-dollar VC fund, sweetened the potential, and Joe offered to meet with me in his London office. A few weeks later, I found myself walking into Joe Gazillionaire's office like it was nothing. I didn't have a polished presentation or a slick strategy. I didn't have an eight-hundred-dollar suit. I didn't even have a prototype. I just walked into that boardroom like I always do: as me.

Now, I'm not one to be easily impressed, as I've said. But I have to say, what Joe had? That was *impressive*. He had an office like you see in the movies. Floor-to-ceiling glass and vintage art decorating the walls. The meeting room was massive. The desks weren't made of particle boards, and why should they? Joe could afford to sit behind real wood, thank you very much. Only King Solomon had more money. I sat at the table in the boardroom, and Joe Gazillionaire walked in. He was smooth and professional, in charge of the room. Billionaires are the kings of the modern world, and Joe was holding court. He was used to people being intimidated, but I wasn't. I wasn't speaking to Superman; I was speaking to a person. I think maybe that was what gave us such instant rapport. I met him on a level that insisted that we were both human. We spoke like people, and it was clear to me right away that he was intrigued.

I presented myself just as I was—as a passionate, self-assured woman who knew what she wanted and what she needed to do to get it. I think now that it was something of a gamble in a way I didn't understand back then. But it was one that paid off. Joe was charmed; he told me that I reminded him of himself, back when he was a younger man. That couldn't be a bad sign. The meeting went off without a hitch, and soon thereafter, I was able to springboard off my meeting with Joe to get a meeting with Dray M. My contact there couldn't believe that on a few weeks' notice, I had sat across the table from Joe Gazillionaire. "That's impossible," he told me. "No one does that." Apparently, the typical process to get a meeting with Joe involved a waiting period of several months. The man has mansions and beach houses all over the world and spends his days traveling between New York, Paris, The Hamptons and London. He's not someone you just call up for brunch. The Dray M execs didn't know *me* very well.

Raising capital was like dancing with the devil; except you're barefoot and the devil is wearing lead shoes. I had no experience, no mentor, and no fear: a wicked combination. But it had gotten my foot in the door. The fundraising process seemed to take forever, but in reality, it only lasted from late 2015 to mid - 2016. I was being battle tested and, so far, I had managed to maintain my sanity, even if only by a thread. It was so grueling and non-stop that I never even noticed my mental health slipping through my fingers like sand through a sieve. The reality of my slipping grip on sanity erupted in a frightful fit of crying one day when I got home. The rumble in my ears was the sound of the walls threatening to squeeze me until I popped. Everything was shaky… except my resolve. I had waited too long, tossed too many co-founders (ugh, that word), and taken too much crap to give up now. My dream was just around on the other side of river. All I had to do was swim past the hungry alligators and make it to the other side with all my limbs intact. Fingers crossed. I did what everyone does when their world is falling apart; hit the rewind button, play it all again, and see what could have been done differently.

I could have chosen better co-… well, you know the word.

I could have studied the process better.

I could have been born in the majority.

I could have been born a boy.

Oh, well. As I imagined a life where I had to down Prozac like Tic Tacs, I accepted that none of what happened was under my control. I had sat across from Life in the Big game and played my hand. All things considered, I had done ok. The weight of the world was on my ever-weakening shoulders. Since I was the one solely in charge of raising capital, I went alone to meet with investors. I sat in a lot of conference rooms across from a lot of men with coffee breath, detailing the specifics of my business model. I called my legal team more than my own mother, never realizing that since they had been hired by the investors, their friends, their advice was biased.

Still, I was close, so close, to the end of this phase. I reassured myself that, once the AI platform was built and we secured our first clients, all would be well. Yeah, naïve. Physically and mentally weaker, my eyes remained fixed on the prize. I was poised to rescue the movie industry from a lot of bad financial decisions. I was certain they would leap at the chance to know, with virtual certainty, what movies would tank and which would soar. So, I determined to press on. Collapsing on the couch one night, licking my wounds and bandaging my ego, I wondered, if I had it to do all over again, would I have taken on a partner from the start? But, with the benefit of hindsight, I landed on the opinion that I wouldn't have it any other way. It was bit like relationships: better to stay single, than be in a shitty one. Wasn't that a movie title? *I Can Do Bad All By Myself*, I think it was. Yes, that was the theme of my business. If I succeed, I would do it alone. And if I failed…

Of course, there was the work: the managing, the meetings, the mayhem. But I was not about to quit. Not now. Hammering out the terms and conditions of the investment deal with the investors was possibly the worst part. It was endless back and forth; investor to me, me to lawyers, lawyers to me and investors, investors to lawyers. It felt like eating spaghetti with a spoon. We hardly got anywhere. In one boardroom, with a cup of bad coffee and room full of suits around me, I felt the tsunami of tears well up in my gut. You know the feeling — when a river of sobs collects and starts rising inside you, parking just behind your eyes. You hold as still as possible. Even the blink of an eye could break the dam and cause a deluge. Then I blinked. *Crap!*

As the tears poured out, the awkward silence was thick as Los Angeles smog. Everyone looked at me like my hair was on fire. I could hear their thoughts. *Look at this woman crying in a meeting over a clause in a contract. She's so weak.* They didn't know the shitstorm I had pushed through from my first interactions with the world. They couldn't feel the pressure that had been placed on me. And they would never relate to the plight of a minority in a world that places you on the starting line of a race, chain an anvil to your ankle, fires the gun, and then laughs when you can't run free like the other racers. The tears had less to do with the contract dispute, which was bad enough, but more to do with the fact that their consciences were so seared, they were unashamed to propose this specific clause. And, to add insult to idiocy, they dared to be shocked that I wouldn't roll over like a puppy begging for a belly rub. They were hot, thick, angry tears. Mercifully someone broke the silence. "Please, stop crying," a bass voice pleaded. "I don't know how to deal with crying women." I wanted to answer, "Please stop being an immature asshole. I'm all out of baby wipes to clean up the crap you put in this contract." Instead, I dried my tears, finished the meeting, went back to my place, and released all the tears I had saved up on the ride home. I was not someone who cried often. I think people who knew me suspected that I had my tears ducts surgically removed. I cried when it seemed I couldn't go to the school I desperately wanted to attend. I cried when I had to say goodbye to my brother for the last time. And I cried at the sight of my parents' bitter tears at losing their son. But not much more of life's adversities were potent enough to pull the tears from my reluctant eyes. But this… this did it.

The lawyers who I paid to represent me even called when I got home and told me I was a fool if I chose not to agree to the proposed contract. "It's a good deal," they said. "You should jump on it," they said. "Don't get lost in the weeds," they said. "This deal is an opportunity of a lifetime," they said. I hung up and cried some more. Despite my bloodshot eyes and embarrassment, I was determined to get what I wanted and deserved. If being a disagreeable person was what it took, I was overqualified for that position. I didn't budge and, in the end, got what I wanted. Me? Cave? I don't think so! I succeeded, though not overwhelmingly. But a win is a win… even if it's an ugly victory. At the end of the first round of funding, I was stunned by my accomplishment. Everyone around me was equally stunned. As I emerged from the dark forest of raising venture capital, I looked back over my shoulder and promised myself not to enter it again. Ever!

After eight months of fundraising, I was ready to get back to my passion and the real reason I wanted to get out of bed every morning. I could now focus on building something I have always been dreaming of — creating a technological innovation that could change an entire industry and perhaps the entertainment world at large. The overwhelming pressure of the public eye remained focused on me. The Belgian media clamored for the story: *First female tech founder to raise over a million in venture capital.* Now I had to deliver. All I wanted was to get to work — to start building the AI I had envisioned and get a product in hand.

SCRIPTBOOK AI

1.2 million U. S. dollars.

1.2 million.

1.2!

The number danced around my head like hummingbirds in the morning. ScriptBook AI, my startup company, was well-funded. For me, and for many people in the tech space in Belgium, it was something out of a dream. If the boys from school could see me now... There have been a handful of female founders in Belgium's tech space who have tried to raise capital for their companies, but they were never able to hit that $1 million standard unlike their male counterparts. I fought my way past the stereotypical limitations placed on women in tech. I overcame the swamp of investors. I had, for now, survived unethical lawyers. And I was certain other women who wanted to get into the tech industry were looking to me as proof that nothing was impossible. Once again, the universe had called on me to set the pace.

I was interviewed live on CNN via Skype from our office in Antwerp. Maggie Lake, the interviewer, put me at ease. Still, my shaky voice revealed that I was in a strange new land of media trying to get my wits about me. A few days later when I saw the picture of me taken during the interview, I noticed how young I looked. With my small, chubby face, I looked like a student just out of university. Genetics had been kind to me. There wasn't a wrinkle on my smooth skin. Which was remarkable, considering the sleepless nights when I laid awake staring at the ceiling praying for death. Even my friends and family noticed that I appeared to be aging in reverse. They remarked that I looked full of life, hope, and possibilities. If they only knew. Determination alone had gotten me past that awful period. Determination… and a bit of luck. Most tech founders pitch their start-ups to hundreds of investors in the hopes of getting a handful. They must cast a wide net if they hope to catch a single fish. I got lucky. I sent a note to Joe Gazillionaire on LinkedIn and that opened all the other doors.

Or maybe it wasn't pure, dumb luck. Maybe I did what others didn't. I went down a divergent path and found the pot of gold at the end of the rainbow. After all, it was a great idea! Whenever I spoke about my "product-in-the-making" to people, they listened to me keenly and were always intrigued, asking questions to further understand the concept behind the AI I was building. I guess the idea sounded sexy and interesting. Much to my surprise, most people don't know much about AI and how it works other than what they see in sci-fi and movies.

Still, ScriptBook AI had no team and not a single client. Most tech startups who raise funds have teams, a minimum viable product, and even paying customers. They are usually seeking funds to scale their businesses. They can show reports about proof-of-concepts, early sales and growth projections. I had an idea and a healthy dose of grit. My company valuation? Their guess was as good as mine. Five million? Fifty million? A billion? I didn't know. The fact that I didn't have a practical valuation had certainly made it hard for me to get a fair deal and it forced the investors to focus more on the protection of their interests. And they did that very well. It was months before I realized how deficient the terms and conditions of the investment agreement were. This doesn't imply that I have regrets. I don't have a single one. Having regrets would mean I was still living in the past. My past was not someplace I wanted to hang out. But I could learn from my mistakes and grow. And I could help other young, female founders who are looking to start a multi-million-dollar tech company. But that would come later. At this point I still had a company to build. And I was damn proud of my idea. I was a reluctant pacesetter and was starting to accept the mantle. The crown was placed on my head without my permission. I cocked it to the side like a rap star and let myself enjoy the moment. It only took two years for another woman in Belgium's tech scene to follow in my footsteps, and raise over a million in venture capital. I wasn't alone anymore, and I liked it. Progress. Pride.

ScriptBook AI was underway. I managed to find time to work while the media kept buzzing around me like a bee at a barbecue. In 2016, a television program in Belgium that featured young entrepreneurs who were rising through the ranks in the technology industry chose me for an episode. It was shot in December. I was also scheduled to appear at the world's largest tech conference called "TechCrunch" in London on the same day of shooting this episode. ScriptBook AI was nominated for a pitch competition at TechCrunch. So, the camera crew from the TV show accompanied me to the event. The hum of the Christmas season was reverberating through London, complete with enough snow to make everyone's selfies look authentic. The streets were blinding bright with Christmas lights and decorations. The camera crew flanked me in front and behind, filming the event. They followed me everywhere, asking me questions. Despite the difficulties I faced before getting to that level, I was proud… and grateful. Toward the end of the filming, we picked a postcard setting to shoot the last scene: me sitting by the river Thames with snow falling around me like tiny angels. I was asked a final quote to close the episode. "Where do you see yourself and ScriptBook 5 years from now?" "I see ScriptBook AI getting listed on the NASDAQ. I want to take my business to the level where I would have an IPO instead of choosing an exit. I want to join the class of the bigger corporations and not sell off my business to a bigger corporation. I want it to serve people around the world regardless of their race, location or socio-economic background. I want Scriptbook AI to change the face of Hollywood. To democratize the film industry and make it accessible for the ninety-nine percent who never get a foot in the door." Ironically, exactly five years later, instead of filing for an IPO, I filed for bankruptcy. But let's not get ahead of ourselves.

Convinced that the marriage between human experience and the super intelligence of AI could be of great benefit to the world, I forged ahead full steam. I believed this included the movie industry all around the planet. From Hollywood to Bollywood, the percentage of movies that flopped would not be made. It would save the film industry a lot of money, lower the cost of tickets (since the winners would not have to cover for the losers) and save moviegoers from a long list of flops available for them to invest their hard-earned ticket money on. Everybody stood to win. The quality of film productions would improve. Voila! The world is a better place.

ScriptBook AI was set to be the custodian of this dream, charged to see it from conception to birth. But was I ready to pay the price to be its midwife? I don't remember asking myself these questions. I wouldn't have known to ask. By combining human's and AI's unique abilities and attributes, ScriptBook AI could help studios, film producers, screenwriters, filmmakers and financiers make good decisions, at least eighty-three percent of the time. Through a carefully built decision support system, using machine learning, deep learning, natura language processing and complex algorithms, ScriptBook AI was set to revolutionize the approach to choosing what movies receive a greenlight.

I had raised enough funds to kick-start the company, and I could also afford such a first-rate team. I gathered a team of twelve PhD level professionals who had track records of being reliable and had great work ethics. They were seasoned analysts, AI wizards, and outstanding mathematicians. Their areas of expertise covered every subfield of AI, ranging from deep learning to reinforcement learning. As we laid the groundwork, we found it was far more complex than we anticipated. Isn't everything, though? Though I had a team of AI gurus on my side, none of them had the slightest idea about what made a great script, or which were a dog! We knew next-to-nothing about screenwriting. We couldn't identify that X-factor that created a box office success script. What is character development or a story arc? What is storytelling? What is conflict and resolution? Or was it just licking a finger and sticking it in the wind? My team and I had all the knowledge we needed to create an AI, but we didn't know how to incorporate this knowledge with what an ideal script should and shouldn't be. We had to educate ourselves in the areas where we were lacking. We gathered different sorts of learning materials, including books, recordings, podcasts, videos, and any other literature that could improve our knowledge in an incremental way. We became students and class was in session day and night for months. We didn't have a product in place, but we learned a lot through deep research. We gathered millions of data points and were able to debunk many Hollywood myths through our research. For example: our research debunked the myth that black lead actors don't do well commercially and that female leads don't do well at the box office. We debunked the notion that blockbusters have a higher return on investment than indie movies (independent movies are far more profitable). We showed that on-screen gender equality hardly improved in over 40-years of movies from 1980 to 2021.

Tiny cracks between the investors and me began to manifest. The investors were growing impatient after the first twelve months without a minimum viable product to show. They assumed my team and I were sitting on our asses doing nothing. They didn't know that we had no asses. We had worked our asses off! I explained the situation to the investors, telling them plainly that they had to be patient. The initial process of building the AI involved research and development. Like all typical R&D, the procedure inevitably required trial and error. I tried my best to be transparent with the investors. I told them every detail they needed to know whether or not it was positive, and I made sure they saw that my team and I were all working ourselves silly. The investors quickly ran out of patience, and their questions came flying at me like mosquitoes by an Alabama swamp. I realized that my investors didn't fully understand what we were trying to build. They thought we were developing a simple app or software that would take only a couple of months to develop. What we were building was far more complex. It was super intelligence, so vast that many of its details were imperceptible to the human eye at first glance. But the investors only spoke one language — returns. So, our delays placed further strains on our relationship.

After about a year, ScriptBook AI succeeded in developing its first algorithm which was a parsing algorithm. This parser would help the AI system to read the script and parse the content of the script. This would allow the system in a later phase to analyze the story according to various parameters and factors. The idea was that the final product would deliver either a favorable or an unfavorable verdict. It would score character diversity, characterization, premise, novelty of the idea behind the plot, genre(s) and so on. To the untrained eye, the algorithm was simple but embedded in it were multifaceted features and interlaced processes that made it capable of making critical decisions. Essentially, we designed a one-of-a-kind, revolutionary system. Despite the many setbacks and the almost insurmountable mountain to climb at the beginning of ScriptBook AI, we achieved what we set out to do.

The tension between me and the investors kept growing thicker. Unimpressed by our accomplishment, they looked at their proverbial watches and asked when the money would be rolling in. Most of them expected to get some of their returns by the first twenty-four months. In this case, that wasn't even close to being feasible. Building an AI system like ours was like constructing a house. First a blueprint is drawn, then the foundation is laid before the actual structure is built. It is an incremental process where each stage is a prerequisite to another. For us to build something solid, we had to take our time without giving in to any pressure. My team and I persevered through late nights, ate leftover morning donuts for dinner, fielded a million research papers and brainstorm sessions, and generated a lot of hope. The investors were unimpressed with the effort that we were putting into creating the product. We envisioned the Mona Lisa of AI systems, and they were treating it like a paint-by-numbers from Walmart. It was safe to say that my investors didn't understand what they had invested their money in. And perhaps, as time went by, as this fact started dawning on them, it became a problem for everyone involved.

THE LION'S DEN

After building our first product features, my team and I thought we were going to be granted some good faith and a little bit of breathing space. I thought my investors would take their heels off our backs and let us work, but I was wrong. They were breathing so hard down my neck I could smell what they had for lunch. For them, moving at a snail's pace, no matter how rigorous or enormous our goals were, was unacceptable. At every board meeting I was obliged to attend; I was bombarded with an avalanche of heated questions. And no matter how hard I tried to answer each of them, explicating each element to the tiniest, indivisible bit, I was never able to satisfy them.

"Do you have any customers yet?"
"Do you have a product / market - fit
"Are there any leads?"
"Why have you not secured any potential clients?"
"Who are your early adopters."
"Why don't you have a sales pipeline?"
"Why are you not doing?"
The questions and criticisms kept pouring out like a surge of water from a broken dam. Of course, the real question was: "When are we going to see some revenue?"

The constant pressure from every angle of my business life was mounting. Stepping into the boardroom was equivalent to entering the seventh circuit of hell. Every time I woke up and remembered I had a meeting slated for that day with my investors, I had to steel my will. I could not let them push me around. If they didn't know where they had put their money, too bad. I wasn't going to rush the AI and roll out something substandard. This was my baby. It needed time to crawl before it walked.

There was a sense of relief whenever I came out of the boardroom with my head still attached to my shoulders. "I survived," I told myself. But the pressure was weighing down on me like an anchor. Their toxic manner and biting words echoed back at me several days after the meeting was over. It played on a loop I couldn't turn off. Then the pressure began to start selling the product before it was done. My team and I were not yet satisfied with the quality of the product and wanted more time to improve it. The investors wanted us to release it into the market at all costs.

In addition to the reality that the AI was not completed, I was caught up in a little dilemma of my own: I wasn't a salesperson in nature. I couldn't sell a thong on Miami Beach. I had zero interest and experience in sales. I was more interested in creating a product than in selling it. So, when the investors started rapping on my door for my first sale, cold feet struck me like a fever. I didn't know what to do or how to go about pitching — especially under duress. We had built a strong and reliable parsing algorithm, but the AI system could only identify genres. Even so, it was perfect. The beta version of the system could read any uploaded script and categorize the genre or genres embedded in it. For instance, if a script titled *Love Kills* was read and parsed by the AI, it indicated the genres in the following way:

Romance: 75%
Drama: 15%
Comedy: 10%
Others: 0%

Producers or script readers didn't need to read through a script before they could recognize what genres it belonged to. In fact, the AI system was more accurate in its analysis than any producer or script reader could ever be. The system was correct ninety-eight percent of the time. However, this product could hardly qualify as the skeleton of the real product we intended to build. It was just too early to start engaging the product with clients. I tried to explain this to my investors during one of our traumatic board meetings. No luck. They wanted what they wanted. Quality be damned.

We still had a long way to go to fit in all the necessary features to create a complete AI system, and we needed more time. But the investors wanted me to pitch. So, I pitched. I sat down in front of my computer with my fingers hovering over the keyboard and my eyes transfixed on the screen. It was a staring contest. The screen won. The email was like a blank sheet of paper, and I was like a best-selling author with writer's block. However, I didn't stop trying. No matter how many times I got up from my desk with the email unfinished, I still came back to it, perhaps with a coffee in hand. I stayed in that space, taking baby steps as much as I could manage and before I knew it, words became sentences — sentences became paragraphs.

I admit I deleted my drafts several times before starting all over again. Even the final draft wasn't terribly impressive. To be completely honest, I didn't think it would garner much response even though I had analyzed each sentence and edited it with the attention to detail of a brain surgeon. The email introduced me as the founder of ScriptBook AI, a tech company dedicated to making life easier for movie studios and production companies. Then I explained that my AI system could read and parse a film script, verify its quality, and predict box office success. I mentioned that I would be in L.A. in a couple of weeks if they wanted to schedule a meeting. Then, reluctantly, I clicked "send."

Pitching emails flew like carrier pigeons to various film production companies and studios, addressed to CEOs and SVPs. I didn't have high expectations about my pitch, but after a few days and weeks, I started getting responses — at the response rate of eighty percent. My first email response came from an executive producer in Los Angeles who expressed a keen interest in the product and was willing to schedule a meeting. Other emails came in. My inbox was bursting. Most of the responses I got expressed instant interest in the product. Astounded with the amount of reception my not-so-good pitch was getting, I felt like I had scored a bestseller. Once I booked a meeting with Yonis Pictures, a major film studio, I bought an airline ticket.

With my meeting itinerary filled in L.A., a city I hated since my late teens, I boarded a plane and headed for the U. S.
Alone!
Me – Daniel.
Hollywood – the lion's den.
When I landed in L.A., I got the same weighted feeling I had all those years ago when I visited the city of angels. I looked left and right. *Yep, still no angels here.* Whenever I travelled to L.A., I always took a flight to New York first, and then I boarded another plane to my final destination. In essence, my layover offered me a chance to sniff the crisp, bustling air of New York City before heading to LA. Since I never looked forward to being in Los Angeles, my stopover at New York lightened the prospect and gave me something to look forward to. New York is everything. Even the crime, filth, rats,

high cost of living, and crushing bureaucracy are not powerful enough to damper its appeal. New York is food and films, cabbies and caviar. It's the one place on earth where urban life meets high society in a perfect mix. And the aroma of that fusion is in the air. Where L.A. is artificially flavored, New York is real, rough, and raw. Yes, New York will beat you down or lift you up. But it will never lie to you. In Los Angeles, they'll pee on your leg and call it rain. So, I was always thankful for a few moments in New York to inoculate myself against the fakeness on the other coast. Los Angeles never appealed to my spirit or my nature, not even when I first encountered it in my late teens. When I left L.A. to return to my home in Belgium all those years ago, I assumed I had left for good. So, when the plane landed and I stepped out into the smog of Los Angeles, my heart went cold inside my chest. Nothing had changed, either with LA, or my feelings towards the city.

The whole place was still a cage of pandering prisoners guised in luxury and entertainment. Hearts ached beneath those painted smiles. Dreams lost or found — it didn't matter. There was a veil of sadness on the faces. People scampered anywhere they could to do whatever tasks were available for them while they sought their breakthroughs. Like bloodhounds, they were all sniffing the ground for their lucky shot, erroneously believing it would free them from the hostile economy. Little did they know that a lucky break would only move them from one prison to the next. And once they were there, they would be required to pony up the one currency a person can spend to be successful in Hollywood: their soul. No matter where I looked, there was underlying fear. People were antsy and nearly in a frenzy. A civilized pandemonium. The left coast was a place where most people chose to ignore their hopelessness, as if it didn't exist. I was too real for this world, which made it even harder for me to develop any affinity with the city. And it wasn't just the city. It was the state itself. I wasn't a big fan of California's scourging sun. Quite nefarious and infamous, it shone from dawn to dusk like an angry god who had been left neglected by his worshippers and were receiving the commensurate punishment. It set a mad, hot temperature each day that wasn't befitting of what I was used to.

I had no doubt in my mind that LA would never be called "home" for me. So despite having meetings scheduled there month after month, I would leave L.A. after a week and return to Belgium. A good number of the film studios in L.A. to whom I had pitched my e-mails had surprisingly expressed interest. My dance card filled up quickly, giving me an average of ten to twelve meetings to attend during my week in LA. Of course, before any of the meetings could be scheduled with the studios, I was mandated to sign non-disclosure agreements. Each of the agreements was legally binding and had monstrous penalties in the event of infringement, some of which had a price tag of millions of dollars. Even if I was tempted to breach this contract of trust for some good reason, a price tag like that was enough to make me think twice about it.

Even today, I think about the weight those non-disclosures carried and sometimes I wonder if breaching them would be worth it. As far as I'm concerned, I would never really know. But one thing I realized early on was that Hollywood was an industry with a heightened sense of paranoia in every way, especially when dealing with strangers coming into their industry. The non-disclosures were like a spell that was cast over every conversation in a place where even speaking the word "trust" was akin to uttering profanity. I wish I could name names. But since I can't, I have opted to use aliases I have given these studios and companies, and leave the rest to your imagination.

The first film studio I visited in LA was Yonis Pictures, definitely one of the biggest in the U. S. and even the world, and for good reasons. I must confess, I was so overwhelmed by everything I saw at Yonis Headquarters, I could understand how it got to be what it was. When I drove onto the premises, a valet approached me and demanded my keys. I had never encountered a valet before, so this was a strange ritual. Was I being robbed? I was hesitant and confused because I had not experienced anything like it before — at home or anywhere else. I confess I had seen it on television. But who would have thought it really happened? I thought valets were reserved for movies or multimillionaires. Even seeing it in film doesn't compare to the first time you hand the keys to an expensive rental car to a total stranger. After all, I could park my car myself; I didn't realize I needed someone to help me do that. In that fleeting moment, I felt like I was lost in a place I didn't belong. However, there were still more surprises waiting for me that day.

I saw a couple of famous actors in the flesh that day just walking around like "normal" people. I had seen some of these actors on several popular TV shows. But seeing them walking to their various shooting sites just like regular people going to their office jobs made me want to pinch myself and confirm if I wasn't in a doctored reality like the Matrix. One of the movie sets was a place I recognized because it was an exact replica of New York. That is one of the seductive charms of Hollywood. It can make you feel like you're on a blustery New York City street with snow crunching under your feet while you're standing under the blazing west coast sun. I felt warm inside just looking at the set. I loved New York City, and the time I spent there exploring the place was unforgettable to me. Certain scenes were etched on my mind forever. So, the moment I saw the site, I instantly knew what I was looking at and my mouth curved into a small smile of nostalgia.

I was totally awed, and I couldn't but gape at the lookalike buildings and familiar streets that I had once seen on TV screens. I had to remind myself time and time again that these things in front of my eyes were real, and I wasn't caught up in some kind of dream. However, that is the right word to describe what I was feeling: a dream. It was as if I had left reality and stepped into a fantasy. It was enough to make me dizzy. At that moment, the whole world seemed to swivel around, lift me up from the surface of the earth, and place me on a cloud of fairy dust. I was in the center of dream world. I found it hard to believe it at first, but as much as my mind argued with my eyes over what it was seeing, nothing could change the fact that everything I saw was truly there and not an illusion. Even today, whenever I close my eyes and remember, I can still feel that surreal moment, and the wonderful feeling vertigo returns. The memories of that "first time" are permanently wedged in the back of my mind.

I shook myself from the fantasy. I was here on business, not to be wowed by Hollywood's ability to erect a magnificent movie set that mimicked reality. Still, this was an incredible opportunity. So, I allowed myself to be a tourist for just a few moments as I walked through the studio's Hall of Fame, staring up at the assembly of pictures in frames that adorned the walls like pieces of artistic prints. The room whispered echoes of triumphant greatness. The squeezed smiles that graced the faces in those frames glinted with self-contented achievement. I was in total awe as I inhaled the enchanting air that floated in the room. Then I advanced to where all the award plaques were gallantly arranged on polished mahogany shelves. They simply magnified the solid achievements of the actors, writers, and directors together with all the behind-the-scenes folks whose hard work made the movie magic happen.

I wanted to take selfies with the awards so I could show my family, but just before I could take the first snapshot, security approached clad in a navy-blue khaki uniform and somber, stone-cold face waving me off, saying matter-of-factly that photos weren't allowed in that room. I widened my eyes in surprise. It was such a bummer for me. Me being me, I pushed back and asked him why snapping a couple of pictures of the larger-than-life photos and plaques should be sanctioned as an abomination. He responded to me with a straight face that the flash from my phone camera would damage the sparkling faces of the plaques. With that, I was almost knocked off my feet and caught myself laughing out loud. I thought it was the most ridiculous response I have ever heard in perhaps the grandest place I had ever been.

It was the perfect example of the Hollywood vibe. They are people who want to be loved, admired, and adored. They want to be chased and photographed. They want to display their prizes for all to see. But taking a photo in the hall was not permitted? I wanted to take those pictures mostly as souvenirs to send to my family and probably to my team back at ScriptBook hoping they might serve up a dose of motivation. But unfortunately, I wasn't allowed to even exist there — much less, take a photo. Welcome to the movie business.

HOLLYWEIRD

walked into the Yonis corporate offices for the first time as the CEO of ScriptBook AI expecting to be met by some lower-level executive. I thought they would appoint some personal assistants, interns, or secretaries to meet with me. I was definitely not thinking they would take me too seriously at first, probably because I was from Belgium — a foreigner with some kind of crazy idea right out of a sci-fi movie and running an unknown tech company that wasn't even in the U. S. Even I didn't think an audience with the big-ups was even remotely possible or necessary. But lo and behold, when I stepped over the threshold of the large conference room, I was met with the sight of eight senior vice-presidents of Yonis Pictures — all men. I wouldn't say I wasn't surprised. In fact, I was a bit perplexed. And I think that is what caused my voice to quake a little when I greeted them and formally introduced myself. There I was, alone at a major motion picture studio with several executives in the boardroom eager to talk to me about the program.

The situation became even more intense when they asked me to present my product on a big screen just at the corner of the room. At the sight of the big dark screen, I went blank like a new sheet of paper. I didn't know until that moment that they were expecting a full-blown presentation from me about my product displayed with the aid of some PowerPoint slides. I didn't even know what to think since I was only prepared to discuss the product. My best hope going into the meeting was that we would schedule a follow-up where a presentation of the AI would take place. I was truly shaken to my core and taken by complete surprise. I guess some surprises are good while others make you stronger. This was a little bit of both. I would get to show my product, but would it work in a way that impressed them?

In this sort of gathering, especially with the caliber of people who were present, surprises were generally a bad omen and, if not managed properly, could send the wrong message. I had to deliver, or there would never be a follow-up meeting. What's more, word might spread that I was all sizzle and no steak, leaving other studios reluctant to waste their time meeting with me. Something inside me sprang into action! I reached into my bag for my laptop and scurried over to the corner to hook it up. Before long, I realized that my stupid laptop wouldn't connect with the big screen for reasons I didn't know. I felt like some evil forces were working against me. It was such a messed-up moment that I am still often embarrassed whenever I remember it. How silly it would look for me to suggest that all eight of these men should drag their chairs together into a tight huddle and lean towards the center of the conference table where I stationed my laptop so that they could peer at the tiny screen. Silly or not… I asked them to gather together. I had no other choice. This presentation was happening. I showed them the charts on my laptop screen as I explained to them that our AI driven script- analysis system could predict the box office success of a movie long before its actual production. The product I showed them was not even a real, ready-to-use product; it was little more than a prototype of what the actual product would look like in a matter of years. That's right, in a matter of years! The product was not even close to being ready at that point, but my investors had urged me not to reveal this critical information to my potential clients. Instead, I was to say. "The product is unfinished but with the rate at which the work is progressing, the product would be completed in a matter of months." I parroted my lines as instructed.

At that juncture, I think I oversold my product and, if you ask me, I felt really bad about it. It didn't feel legit. It wasn't me. Perhaps you can catch the "plastic parasite" just by stepping foot in Hollywood. I was behaving in a manner I abhorred in them. But I had to please my investors and, since the deed was done, it was pointless for me to backtrack again. In business, it is better to look forward into what is possible in the future or what can be accomplished. Another one of the pressing reasons I oversold the product to them was because I felt intimidated by the host of eight senior vice-presidents who had freed up their time just to meet me. I wanted to keep up the standard I had unconsciously set for myself. I wanted to continue holding their interest in the product.

In hindsight, it might have been easier to meet with a number of lower-level executives who were a bit more impressionable and less savvy. This silly setup of men in power suits squinting to see a small laptop screen would have been more palatable if it has been a group of interns who were obliged to report the outcome of the meeting to their respective bosses. I was only a young woman who had stepped into that elegant and luxurious conference room and been besieged by seemingly sophisticated and influential men. And I had a rough prototype of a product that was not even sellable at that moment, though I tried my best to make it look sellable. I told them that the current available features of my product could help evaluate movies and detect their genres and MPAA ratings based on the content of the scripts. At least that much was true.

They were quite surprised and even excited about it, and they kept asking me, "It can do that based on just the script?" Their mouths were open and their eyes wide as though I was divining what they had eaten for breakfast or telling them the name of their high school sweetheart. I answered their questions in the affirmative and further explained that all they had to do was upload the scripts as PDF files and, within a few minutes, the AI system would read, parse, and analyze the scripts. I promised that, at the end, it would give its prediction on the box office success or failure, depending on the overall quality of the storyline. There and then, the executives made it known to me that they were quite pleased with what I was offering. They also disclosed that my AI program was precisely what they needed at that time in their business. They confessed that, at the early stages of any movie production, they did not have a good, objective and reliable tool to help in their decision-making process. *Tell me something I don't know.*

I already knew that the movie industry was putting out dogs that barely covered the costs of production. But I also knew that they were wasting countless hours moving film projects along in the process called development hell — usually scripts that didn't have a chance of box office success. Yet they spend millions upon millions of dollars only to later decide not to run with it for some reason. There are so many factors to consider when deciding if a movie project is worth the studio's while. The act structure of the script, the emotional development and journey of the characters, the plot line, the presence of at least one powerful plot twist, the suspense the script builds, the arcs in the story, the universality of the themes and so on and so forth, have to be carefully analyzed. Movies, unlike books, must have broad appeal. They must find a way to reach the widest possible audience without losing the basic theme of the film.

That was the basis of my concern about running scripts through ScriptBook AI. We had planned to have many points of analysis. The features it currently had were not enough. In order to arrive at the best prediction, the AI's work needed to be based on the many parameters that help to assess a movie's potential. The higher the number of parameters provided, the higher the chances of getting an accurate prediction for each movie script submitted for analysis. That is the way the system worked. That is how an AI works. It needs data and lots of it. The more data it has the better it does its job.

The SVPs asked me to test run my product with a couple of movies they hadn't released yet — for free, of course — and I agreed to the arrangement, even though I was terrified to do so. With the way everything had progressed that day, both the good and bad parts, it would have been a bit awkward if I had refused. Besides, I didn't want my team and my investors back at home to realize that I had flown all the way to L.A. and met with the higher-ups of Yonis Pictures but had turned down the offer of a project. So, I swallowed hard, straightened up, and started to make the necessary arrangements. My first step was to relay my progress and the ensuing challenge to my team back home. I was thrilled to be able to report to them that things were going rather well and that I had experienced a not-too-bad-for-a-start reception from the Senior Vice Presidents of Yonis Pictures. My team was elated and encouraged as I thought they would be. But, when I reported my progress from the Yonis meeting to the board, the reaction was less than enthusiastic. I became exasperated when certain members of my board began to ask me the amount of money Yonis Pictures was going to pay for the test analysis we were going to run for them. I was so pissed! Didn't they understand that this test run was a loss leader and would likely blow their socks off enough to actually get a deal? Or did they know nothing about how these things worked?

With such a massive head start with a fabulous and large potential client, and with many more meetings on my calendar, all they could think about was money we had not earned yet. It was so ridiculous to me. The investors wanted to count the money from their cut of the sale of a product that they knew was not even finished. They were the ones who had advised me to tell the client the product was done when it truly was not. Did they also expect that I would accept a check for services knowing I had an incomplete product to offer? Did they know what it had taken for eight Senior Vice-Presidents to agree to meet me?

I tried to explain to the investors that it would be wiser to secure the client's trust by offering them free trials before engaging them in real business. We needed to establish ourselves in this hardened industry. That's just business... something I assumed they understood. I thought they would be thrilled. After all, there were other people with better connections who had sought that kind of opportunity and had been refused several times. I had done better than getting my foot in the door. I got my butt in the chair! And I had managed to pitch an idea well enough to pique their interest despite being not even close to having an end product. Still, by divine intervention, they had opened their doors to me and granted me audience. It was rare. Really rare.

But my board members were nearsighted and greedy. They never saw the steps toward success as a journey. They wanted to go from zero to sixty in each encounter. It seemed like I was interacting with zombies who just wanted their next bite of human flesh. They lacked any sense of imagination, creativity, process, or networking. They were unexplainably myopic to these things that seem, to you and me, to be fundamentals in business. This conversation was representative of the kind of dialogue I had to suffer through during my interactions with the board. Our board meetings usually played out the same way each time. I would rush in excited and they would pull out their blow darts and pop my balloons. I would come crashing to the ground, and they would laugh their heads off as if they didn't connect my entrepreneurial victory with their profits. Yes, metaphorically speaking, that is how each meeting went.

It is not a surprise that I began to struggle with my job. What I called success; they called treading water. What they called sales, I called lying. We did not speak the same language. Hell, we weren't even on the same planet. That was why each time I left a meeting, my spirits were always down no matter how hard I tried to pacify my investors. Although the relationship I had with my investors was depressing, and I sometimes crawled to my bed with the whole of me feeling spent, I was still focused on the endgame. I knew where the company was going. And despite not being as functional as I wanted it to be, ScriptBook AI worked! That had to be enough.

I wanted to run the free analysis of the Yonis Pictures scripts using our system. But I was anxious at the same time because our system was just a prototype that was only able to use a single input factor to run the analysis. And I was really concerned that if our predictions were wrong, every hope we had or ever would have with our system and its potential would be canceled. But we undertook the analysis. Yonis Pictures loved the AI and wanted to take it for a spin on a huge blockbuster movie they had coming out — *Travellers,* a space movie with two of Hollywood's biggest stars. I didn't even mind that they asked me to evaluate the movie for free. The movie was set to be released in December, and we predicted its box office sometime between October and November. Using the prototype that we had, we predicted $118 million dollars for the movie and eventually by the time the movie was released, it rolled in $100 million easily. The executives were so overjoyed. They were satisfied that our formula for the prediction had been accurate. They also mentioned two other blockbusters, *Skinburns* and *Fairy Dusters*, so I threw those in for free as well. And ScriptBook AI came through like gangbusters. It was unbelievable — the analysis. I couldn't believe it.

Creating an AI is similar to giving birth. You know you were responsible for it. But it is much more magnificent and beautiful than you could have ever imagined. And your pride overflows. ScriptBook AI exceeded our expectations. Still, we had quite a way to go to make it all it could be. This was no time to spike the ball, hang up our cleats, and place our trophies on the shelf to be admired. Instead, it was time to dig in and really get to work. Luck favors the prepared. And if we took our foot of the gas now, our good luck might run out!

As I talked with my data scientists about everything that was going on, I expressly informed them that the whole performance of the AI in analyzing scripts so far was mostly luck. I had to be sincere about the system's limitations because it had not been fully developed yet. It was still in its infancy with some serious growing up to do. We were crawling. But soon we would walk, run, and then fly! I didn't want an ounce of our success in landing on their targets to be based on chance. At this point in our development, beginner's luck was in full manifestation. It had been little more than good fortune that I got the meetings in the first place. Then to have the first film run through the system on my laptop and produce an accurate result was a gift from the technology gods. The team was jumping for joy. I hated to temper their excitement — I felt it too. But as the CEO, it was my job to acknowledge what was at stake. One mistake, and all our victory dances would end and our hopes at rolling out the AI program in a big way would vanish. I had a frank discussion with the team during which I informed them that we needed to further develop the system and upgrade it significantly. I didn't want to ever meet with someone again without the full assurance that the product was everything it could be. I had to be able to put away doubts and headaches about its performance and just focus on selling. I had nerves of steel, for sure. But each meeting ground me down until I started to feel fearful. Anxiety got the better of me each time I went to meetings, and I was always stressed about everything. I was always in this state because the system was still in its early stage of development, a prototype, a skeletal product at best, and I was really paranoid that it could fail us.

In the heat of all that, I still had sizeable correspondences with the press, and I confidently told them that our system was capable of analyzing any film project that is brought to it. My confidence in front of such press coverage was strange. I was surprised with myself as I defended the ability of our system regardless of its current condition. Not that the system was bad, the parsing algorithm was extremely solid, but the overall product was not fully developed. It was like giving a child a car to drive or a horse to ride. It only made predictions based on MPAA ratings and genres, and this wasn't adequate enough to assess how great a script was or how it could contribute to the success of the movie in the box office. How the AI system managed to be so accurate in its prediction was beyond me even though I was its chief creator.

Curious to see how the technology would perform in real-world conditions, Yonis Pictures invited ScriptBook AI to run a proof of concept—essentially a long-term trial—applying its analysis to a slate of upcoming film projects as well as movies the studio had released over the previous five years. The goal of the

Proof of Concept was to identify the movies that hit and those that flopped. The results of this trial would be able to confirm our AI's accuracy to Yonis Pictures.

I was prepared to talk to Yonis Pictures and explain why we needed a bit of time to do that. But the board got wind of Yonis Pictures' request. They approached me and demanded that I move forward with the Proof of Concept. I urged them to use caution, told them that the move was hasty, and explained how their actions could cause a backlash. The AI was still in a premature state, and the results of the Proof of Concept could turn out extremely disappointing to Yonis Pictures. However, they shook their heads in disapproval and insisted that they wanted me to talk to Yonis about the initiative. My hands were tied.

So, we undertook the Proof – of – Concept, and I was quite pleased that we had the team we had. They pushed themselves to levels of excellence that surpassed anything they had done before. The preliminary stage of the whole Proof of Concept - operation lasted for about six months, and during those six months, we were able to work hard and come up with a better version of our product. The cost was many sleepless nights and many gallons of coffee. But the team and I got it done. I was able to experiment with over ten thousand movies within those six months, and it was not until after those months that the real work began. This blessing-in-disguise delay on Yonis Pictures' side stemmed from the careful process of drafting and finalizing non-disclosure agreements and proof-of-concept contracts.

We worked hard, long, and fast, to get the Proof of Concept completed just so that the Hollywood execs could place us on the back burner. That is one of the other sins of the Hollywood machine. It often grinds to a halt just when you are on the cusp of something great. I thought of all the actors and actresses who were told to drop everything and rush in for an audition only to wait months without hearing anything. I could relate! Everything in Hollywood was cursed with an extremely slow process because there were so many people involved in every decision. Bosses here and bosses there. And just when you think you've reached the person at the top of the food chain, you learn he has to check in with yet another boss.

It was the worst sort of bureaucracy on planet earth, but I realized very early that I could use it to my advantage. The prolonged procedure of weeding through the red tape afforded me and my team the opportunity to improve our system even more. We just kept running, adding more features to the system that would enable it to make more detailed and well-versed analysis about several aspects of a movie script, thereby improving the accuracy of its predictions. At the end of those six months, we had a much better version of the product than even we anticipated. There was a huge performance boost by the time we experimented on the other movie scripts. I could feel some of my fear and anxiety about the AI lifting from me. Without an iota of doubt, it was a vast improvement over the alpha version of the product we had worked on earlier. The more data we fed the AI system, the more intelligent it became. The more intelligent it was, the better its output. The logic was pretty much straightforward. Still, it was thrilling to watch it in action. It was like viewing fireworks. You know what's going to happen. But you keep your eyes glued to the sky for the next pop and flash. At the end of our hard and extensive work, it turned out that the system had gotten the hang of what it was meant to do. It performed well beyond expectations. Among other amazing things, it could identify the movies that did great at the box offices and the ones that had flopped in a tremendous fashion because it could easily predict the exact amount of box office revenue that a movie would rake in after its production.

Honestly, I was surprised and proud at the same time. My team and I couldn't have been happier that we had found the secret sauce to the movie industry. If there was an elixir for the ills of the movie industry across the world, then it was our product. Though I was stunned in the midst of everything, I felt like a scientist who had found a cure to a lethal epidemic. My expectations were high that every executive in the industry would pounce on this technology and essentially guarantee themselves hit after hit after hit. After all, moviegoers had a big appetite for new films. After seeing a great movie, they always want to see another. And the only cure for a lousy film is to plunk down your credit card and buy a ticket to a fantastic one. If SriptBook AI could ensure that studios only released their best work, they could take the entertainment world to a new level. My heart and eyes were filled with delusions of grandeur. Once ScriptBook AI cornered the market in Hollywood, the possibilities were endless. Next stop, Broadway? Books? Who knew!

In essence, ScriptBook AI had in place the features that mattered when it came to predicting the financial returns of movies long before production. Instead of relying heavily on lucky stars, intuition, gut feelings, or even past experience, the AI was able to see the future and provide an accurate prediction within eighty to eighty-five per cent of the actual box office take. Who wouldn't want to play those odds? I was confident that ScriptBook AI could take on any film project and make the correct forecasts as intended. That is why my demeanor transformed and I became so much more at ease even at the time we officially started the Proof of Concept. I didn't have any reason to stay awake in bed wondering and worrying what would happen if something went wrong. I knew ScriptBook AI had the best product in its niche, even in the entire world, and I was willing to show it off to anyone who would sit still long enough to listen.

I could not have been prouder as the CEO of a tech company. During that time as well, we were hounded by various media outlets both in the U. S. and in Europe that reportedly favorably on the AI. They became keenly interested in our product and closely monitored the progress we made. There was CNBC, The Guardian, The Times, Variety and so on, who followed us at every step we took and reported everything we did to the rest of the world. Consciously or subconsciously, they built a sort of expectation around our product; the more media exposure ScriptBook AI got, the higher the expectations that was placed on it. Even at the early stages of media coverage, some people doubted that the product even existed, thinking it was just myth or a wishful idea. It didn't take long before they were proven wrong. But it wasn't just the media who were watching us. Inevitably, we had several competitors sprouting up here and there, especially in the U. S. Anything you can do will generate copycats who think they can do it better. They worked around the clock to outfox and beat us in our field. But they couldn't come close to creating what we had. Besides, we had a sizeable head start. We were the best out there and the undisputed champion of that sort of AI system.

One of the many reasons we were able to claim that we were the best was because, as I had told every member of my team, there were two ways to play this game — take the easy road or walk the tough one. The easy road was filled with shortcuts. I told them to take the latter — the tough road. It might be longer, harder, and filled with more obstacles, but it was worth all the pain and the time spent when you end up with a final product that excels above all others.

Luckily, we started with the most difficult part of building such a robust AI tool: the parsing algorithm. It was one of the key ingredients to the high-quality, inimitable status of our AI system. Thankfully, our competitors had not realized this priceless philosophy. They were working from a completely different methodology and, as such, placed ScriptBook AI at an automatic advantage. Some of our competitors were money-driven rather than product-driven, so they were content to snatch the low hanging fruits. They performed their analysis based only on social media statistics, the names of cast members, guestimates about star power, and marketing reach to make box office predictions. It was a valiant try on their part, and I can understand why they went in that direction. But those criteria were not nearly enough. It turned out they needed more than just a few factors, however significant, if they wanted to make a strong accurate point of view on a movie's box office. At some point, they would need to go beyond the surface elements of the movie, and that meant examining the story itself. The truth of the matter was that even a great actor, wonderful director, and breathtaking set cannot cover for a garbage script.

For us, the script was the thing! I discovered this connection between a powerful script and box office success during the earliest days of ScriptBook AI. This connection formed the basis of my work from day one. The script became critical. I set out to manufacture an AI that could read a story and determine from the words whether its characters were strong. It could parse out their stereotypical and dynamic emotions. Programming that feature was a complex task to undertake. But it had to be done. Without it, we would have been on the base level along with all the other competitors. We decided to go ahead with handling the most difficult R&D phase first, before we added the low hanging fruits of the model thereafter. I must admit that this character-analysis feature really gave us an edge. It put us at an advantage and gave us many months, perhaps years of advantage over others in our field. That one focus had the power to score a significant achievement for us. Unsurprisingly, some of our competitors were humble enough to approach us, inquiring about our parsing algorithm, and even a possible merger.

Meanwhile, back at the board of directors… The members of the board only spat out their disapproval about the decisions I had made. I couldn't see a single person attempting to inquire about or understand why I made those decisions. It was frustrating that none of them had the vision to see that what ScriptBook AI was achieving at that time was revolutionary. Even without an order in hand, it had proven itself and was starting to make waves. All deep-rooted institutions are like the hide of elephants — tough and impenetrable. Even lions in the wild steer clear of elephants. ScriptBook AI was just a young lion. The company represented, essentially, a symbol of radical change in the movie industry. We were attempting to shape a more than one hundred-year-old mainstay filled with fragile egos resistant to change. This was bigger than money, though the potential for it to make millions could not be denied. This was about improving moviemaking forever. ScriptBook AI could be the definitive tool that ensures bad movies were a thing of the past.

We were making history. The Blind Board of Bozos could not see that. What could be sadder than to be on the cusp of etching your name in entertainment history and completely miss it. But for them it was all trees — no forest. I was playing the long game. If we took our time and did it right, we would set a new industry standard and be the "go-to" organization much like Central Casting was when they went from a small organization in 1925 to the leader in casting. ScriptBook AI was destined to be a household name in the industry.

Though I had painted the vision for the board of directors many times, they still did not realize that I had deliberately made the company a long-term venture. My focus was not fixed on short-term or immediate gains but on the big picture. I was flying at 35,000 feet in my business philosophy, and they were pecking on the ground like pigeons. Ensconced in their position that ScriptBook AI needed to sign a studio right away, they did not understand that in a long-term venture, you do not expect profits so quickly. But my message fell on deaf ears and their demands for signed contracts with movie studios grew louder until it was deafening. Still, I was patient. I decided I would try again.

At the next board meeting, I reminded them as plainly as I could that we had already won. The AI had proven itself and was still being improved. We had caught the eye of a major studio. And we were in the eyes of the media who were watching and chronicling our success. The name ScriptBook AI was mentioned in a Wall Street Journal Report on the Computational Creativity Market next to big names like Microsoft, IBM, and Google as major computational creativity suppliers. We were in a good position; this was not the time to do something foolish or run ahead of our success. Our actions and inactions were under the tight scrutiny of the public. What number of sales could have positioned ScriptBook AI in the same manner? You do not build a company on a wing and a prayer. Business is all about fundamentals and growth over time. ScriptBook AI was a business that had staying power. In a couple of years, it would be leaps and bounds better than it was. It needed to have time and space to develop. Besides, we were establishing relationships and networks; these take time. I may as well have been speaking Mandarin. They either didn't agree or couldn't understand. Either way, I wasn't getting anywhere. But the evidence was everywhere for them to see. The Yonis Pictures Proof of Concept, for example, spanned eighteen months from start to finish. That alone should have given them a clue that this was a slower investment than they were used to.

It felt insane going back and forth with Yonis Pictures. We took one step forward and two steps back. And we were held down by the disclosure agreement whose penalty fee was up to several millions of dollars. Our hands were tied. We had also been told that, if the studio decided they wanted to sign a commercial deal with ScriptBook AI, they would not collaborate with us all the way from Belgium. That invariably meant that we had to establish a base in the United States. We would have to pack up our gear and potentially our team, and move our entire operation to the U. S.

AUDREY HEPBURN

f I was going to please paying customers, I needed more than what we had developed. Whether or not this was my hubris all along, I didn't know. But I was sure of myself and the possibility of making this idea materialize. The thought of a finished product made my tired bones come alive. I knew that there were AI systems that could predict how much a movie would make in its opening weekend. However, AI that predicted box office success solely based on the written script, was new. Researchers from first-rate Universities like MIT, Harvard, Wharton, and Oxford studied production and marketing budgets of movies, reactions and engagement of movie enthusiasts on social media before the release, star power of the members of the cast, producers, and directors, as well as other factors to predict the box office success the movies would have. However, most of these projections were not as accurate as the film industry would have wanted. And they always came after the movie's production. Too little, too late.

None of the predictive models gleaned data from the quality of the script or storyline. Most people prefer great stories over just a great cast. All aspects of film production are important to the success of the movie; however, our research showed that the quality of the storytelling has an inherent predictive value. The story should take precedence, not just because it's mostly what movie enthusiasts want but because it is the foundation of every movie. The truth of the matter is that most film projects in Hollywood are greenlighted into production based on a hunch, and the statistics prove that this method fails most of the time. Hollywood still employs an ancient methodology when greenlighting movies using the very technical tools of gut feeling to make multimillion dollar or billion-dollar decisions. This kind of subjectivity led to box office failure most of the time. ScriptBook AI would be the industry's messiah. Or so I thought. I was obviously wrong. But I didn't find that out until much later.

The wheels were rolling on the company. I was in my glory. I was doing what I somehow instinctively knew since those school days when I stood alongside the boys in school who thought I shouldn't be there. The itch I always had for technology and innovation was being satisfied. ScriptBook's website was a thing of beauty. The design was fresh and engaging. I wanted the website to speak to writers and producers and filmmakers and studios in a unique way. I asked our designer to craft the site to answer the questions they dared not ask about why the movie industry was so variable and unpredictable. I wanted the website to say that ScriptBook AI could predict. And it would predict. The highlight of the site was a pixelated image of Audrey Hepburn. The original tagline was:

ScriptBook
AI Driven Script Analysis and Box Office Predictions

Our mantra was on every landing page, on all our promotional materials, and on every presentation. The press picked it up and ran stories. The delight of seeing "ScriptBook AI" popping up here and there in news reports and in Hollywood circles was thrilling. People were talking about us even though we were on the other side of the world in a small town most Americans never heard of. We were still debating whether or not to move our headquarters to the US. But the buzz was building.

The offers started rolling in like waves to speak at industry conferences and film festivals. These high-profile events grew my muscle as a public speaker, though that was something I never aspired to be. Still, I said yes because they represented opportunities to get the word out about ScriptBook AI from a commercial perspective. But I also talked about AI & tech in general and the ways it impacts industries. I was in heaven. And I was growing as a speaker and marketeer.

One of the earliest invitations had me on a plane to Germany for Berlin International Film Festival. It was a crisp February day. And I was pumped to be in the thick of the vigor that film festivals bring. This one was particularly exciting because the organizers seemed to understand that technology was becoming a major player in the film industry, moving from the exception to the rule in moving making. And there I was with my finger on the pulse of a revolutionary AI product that would ensure only the best films were made. The energy in the room was palpable. FilmNation, LionsGate, MGM and all the other big companies were there. CEOs of major Hollywood companies gave keynote speeches about changes in the industry. Anyone who was anyone was there. *I* was there. Did that mean I was someone? It seemed so.

I was allowed to present ScriptBook AI in a large conference room of industry executives, film financiers, screenwriters, and independent producers. My demo offered screenshots of the product and an explanation of the technology. I knew I was talking to a room full of creatives about a product that could pick a winner better than they could. That was like talking to a room full of doctors about robot-surgeons that could perform surgeries faster, cheaper, and with fewer medical errors. They looked terrified at the prospect as they imagined their own brand of "genius" reduced to ones and zeroes. But I hoped they could see… I hoped I could show them that this was a tool like any other tool that would make their work more efficient and, frankly, more lucrative. But I could see their brains slowly closing in front of my very eyes as they reasoned, "If we let AI into this space, it's going to ruin the industry." What they were really saying was that they were afraid and didn't know what their place would be.

For as much as we associate Hollywood with innovation, the truth is that there is an old-guard mentality there. Once your name has been established, preserving it becomes your highest priority in life. For example, I can imagine them shaking in terror that their past decisions on movies might be put through ScriptBook AI and shown to be the dogs they ended up being at the box office. I tried my best to explain why this was what they needed. But it was much like telling a four-year-old why the doctor with the needle was doing a good thing. *Yes, honey, I know this stranger wants to plunge a long needle into your flesh. Just trust me. It's good for you."*

Call me optimistic. I thought the power of my presentation could temporarily turn off the switch on their ego and turn on the switch of reason, judgement, and business savvy. More good movies would be made, and they would save millions. But the switches in their heads were rusted from years of neglect. I could not toggle them from ego to enterprise. We all are presented with opportunities to be better. That sometimes comes through education. But it often comes through channels that feel like criticism. ScriptBook AI was a chance for them to be better executives, better star producers, and better Oscar-winning directors. Actors would have better movies to appear in, and the public would shed that underlying fear that their expensive movie ticket would result in a subpar experience. Only the movie critics could really have a beef with ScriptBook. After all, if all the movies were good, what would they have to write about. But I wasn't too worried about that. Critics always find a way to critique. They could find fault with a baby kitten. *That baby kitten was so sickly sweet, I could feel the cavities forming in my mouth. The "mew, mew, mew" was so grating, I'd rather be listening to fingernails on a chalkboard.*

The industry bigwigs had painted my technology as a villain in their story, and I had to find another way to get through to them. Shocking, given the fact that events like film festivals and film industry markets were designed to give disruptive technology a forum to show how they can improve the film business. But ScriptBook AI was, apparently, too disruptive for them. Still, I wasn't going to give up. I would help them become more successful in spite of themselves. I just had to figure out what their love language was! The general public on the other hand, got it instantly. They seemed to understand what ScriptBook AI could do. After I spoke, I couldn't exit the stage because a crowd of excited people had formed who wanted to talk to me about ScriptBook. One after another, they shook my hand, asked me questions, and communicated their excitement. Some were struggling screenwriters who saw ScriptBook as a way to improve their craft. Others were independent producers who couldn't afford to waste millions of production dollars on a dud. The line grew, and I tried to answer all their questions. The primary sentiment was, "I know I need this, but I don't understand how it works." Those conversations helped me refine ScriptBook's mission. The events were always followed by a barrage of emails. My inbox was bursting with questions about cost, licensing, utilization. Some even sent scripts to be analyzed! But the overwhelming concern everyone had was the desire to understand the technology better. I realized I needed an educational component to the marketing plan if I was going to be able to get past the natural doubts that arise from uncertainty. If I didn't educate these professionals to the changes in their industry, they would get swept away. The future was unfolding. Rejecting ScriptBook AI would not stop them from being affected by the intrusion of AI on film and television as it was doing on every other industry in the world.

The invitations to speak were a confirmation that ScriptBook AI was wanted. But the response of the attendees told me that it was also needed. Then… there was the fight. Okay, we'll call it a heated disagreement. I sat on a panel at a film industry market in Cannes that had experts on either side debating the issue of whether or not technology was a hindrance or a help to the TV and film industry. It started of civil enough with the obligatory pleasantries and nods of affirmation. But the temperature rose very quickly as hardliners felt their judgement and special gifting in their work was under attack and the innovators felt stifled by the old guard blocking entry to new ideas. Had it gone on a minute longer, I suspect panelists would have come to blows in a display sure to bring everyone's smart phone out to catch the action and post on social media.

Such events left me fearful of the Q&A session that followed the discussion. People had strong opinions on either side of the issue. When they got their turn at the microphone to speak, there weren't many Qs… mostly As. Actually, mostly angry or pointed tirades at whatever side opposed them. Every five-minute-long Q&A lasted 30 minutes. Half the room had questions for me! The few who weren't angry were confused. They wondered why the industry was keeping this AI in the dark. They demanded answers. And I was the schoolteacher, attempting to educate the world on AI driven script analysis. Actually, I was more like a rock star handing out autographs. I attended film festivals in Zurich, Toronto, Berlin, Venice, Cannes, Karlovy Vary, etc. The best of the best trotted around the globe as I did and met in these big venues to discuss changes in TV and film. Interesting people. I was certain that there would be a spark that would set ScriptBook ablaze.

In the meantime, a big part of my job was wading through airports to go to venues and then wading through the scores of people waiting their turn in line to talk to me about ScriptBook AI. In the process, I moved from teacher to rock star to therapist as I listened to the screenwriters who shared their pain with me about their scripts. I felt their pain. They all told me the same stories; all that changed were a few minor details. They were all struggling financially. They were all weary from trying to get a foot in the door with the big movie houses. They had all been carrying scripts for years and years, hoping to get them picked up. Some literally had the scripts on their person. They had all been the recipient of empty promises from talent agencies and Hollywood filmmakers. They were certain that ScriptBook would give them a competitive edge by providing a concrete and objective analysis of their script which they could share to enhance their pitch. They saw ScriptBook as a way to legitimize their art and expertise. With ScriptBook AI, their pitches would be elevated from just an esoteric and subjective recounting of their story to a highly technical, well-analyzed look at the market, demographics, and potential box office returns. ScriptBook was the answer they had been waiting for. And they saw me as their fairy godmother.

I would get on the plane preoccupied with both the economics and politics of Hollywood. It was its own kind of Wall Street-style biosphere. Except, in Hollywood, the gap between the one percent and the ninety-nine percent is even wider. There were literally a handful of directors, and a handful of production companies that seemed to control the majority of Hollywood's film business. Those bigwigs were earning a shitload of money while the rest slung plates of meatloaf and corn in restaurants to pay the rent and keep the lights on. Some of the people I met worked three or four jobs because they had been in the game so long, they had a family to feed. One crappy job just wouldn't do.

Thousands upon thousands, were unknown, struggling, and desperate. After pouring years and years into a script, they would watch it sit and rot on their desks, pages beginning to curl, darken, and fray along the edges. It's like watching over a hospice patient. I knew some of those scripts were masterpieces. But they would never see the light of a Hollywood stage. The reality of this disparity changed me. Deeply. And it led to a big change in our company's mission. I glanced at our website and realized that, in light of all this new information, the tagline was insufficient. We needed something more. Something different. After all, the homepage was graced with an image of the legend herself, Audrey Hepburn. I had a new appreciation for the mission of the company. So, we needed a tagline that soared. Then it came to me:

ScriptBook:
Democratizing the business of storytelling through the art of AI.

It was a winner.
It resonated.
It stood up on two legs, hands on hips, and sashayed!

I was no longer merely an entrepreneur. I was a brand ambassador… a town crier… a prophet. Some prophets are hoisted on the shoulders of the crowd and cheered as they are marched through the city. Some prophets are stoned. And some… well… some have a cross waiting for them.

THE BLACK LIST

The nights were long and the days were hard. But it was a good "hard." It was the kind of "hard" like an intense workout that send endorphins racing through your body and popping off your skin. It was hard like a strenuous climb up a steep mountain that taxes your body beyond belief until your brain screams you can't take another step, but the idea of the panoramic views at the summit keeps you pushing. It was hard like birthing a child. The labor pains have you panting and pushing and just when you think you have nothing left to give, a miracle is born. But there was no baby waiting for me at the end of this labor.

Building technology that could democratize Hollywood was like a spiritual crusade for me. It wasn't about movies at all. Not really. It was about leveling the playing field and giving everyone a fair shot at making their art and presenting it to the world. I was up against a dictatorship — an oligarchy — and seeking to dismantle a hundred years of nepotism and privilege. Me… David. Hollywood… Goliath. Except in my case, instead of a few smooth stones to bring my giant down, I carried a damn big boulder: ScriptBook AI. My heart was pure and my mission was clear. I was determined to bring about change. ScriptBook AI wasn't going to be another startup that created valuable technology and only licensed it to the power players in an industry. I wanted to find a way to make it easily accessible to anyone. Everyone! My loyalty was to the ninety-nine percent: the poor screenwriters, obscure producers, and independent filmmakers. In the end, it was my largesse that spelled my doom.

It was 2017 and our team set off with this new mission in mind. Before then, it was all about enterprise. I simply wanted to sell my technology through big licensing fees. I saw the dollar signs sparkling in my eyes. It never crossed my mind that there was an entire substrate beneath the high-powered executives. They were the foundation of the industry because the existence of the "nobodies" made the "somebodies" elite. I had a new goal to help the women and men who were lowest on the totem pole. I shared my revelation with my team, and we knew the road would be long and difficult. Changing Hollywood is like turning an ocean liner in the middle of the sea. There are no hairpin turns. It takes an hour to steer the ship in the opposite direction. This would not be a quick process, especially since Hollywood wasn't quite ready to admit it had a problem and, even if it did, wouldn't have a clue about the solution. Henry Ford, founder of Ford Motor Company, is attributed with saying, "If I had asked people what they wanted, they would have said faster horses." There's no proof Ford said this, but whoever did was a bloody genius. It's true.

Knowing you have a problem, as they say, is half the battle. The other half, however, is knowing what solution truly solves your problem. But Hollywood worked on a different system. It didn't follow science. It followed stardom, lucky breaks, gut feelings, and other very non-technical muses. Innovators see what the touchy-feely crowd can't see.

Perhaps I should have known that attempting to shift the power balance and purse strings on Hollywood executives would be met with fierce resistance. After all, most people are tuned into one radio station in life: WIFM — What's In it For Me. They saw ScriptBook as a threat to their future fortunes. But it wasn't. Their limited thinking suggested that there was one pie, and they were enjoying their slice of it. My thinking was to enlarge the pie! There were enough pieces for everyone, and the slices they had enjoyed for years would get bigger. Hell, there could be more pies! There was enough wealth to share if Hollywood wasn't losing billions on films nobody wants to see.

But Hollywood was their kingdom. They were oligarchs who had gotten fat on their brand of voodoo that kept the decision-making power in their tiny community. Knocking their crowns off their heads would not be easy. They would fight back. I, on the other hand, was possessed with a noble cause to empower the creatives in the moviemaking business. It occupied my dreams, both sleeping and awake. I was making a little film of my own that played in my head. In my file, the ninety-nine percent rise up, storm the ivory tower, and dethrone their oppressors: the one percent. But Hollywood yuppies and execs with their expensive suits, personal chefs, and twelfth floor offices had their hands on the steering wheel, and they weren't about to cede control to me. Beyond that, I had employees to pay and investors to satisfy with fat returns on their money. At times, they felt like competing concerns. At other times, they seemed completely aligned. It was time to make a phone call.

I reached out to Franklin Leonard, founder and CEO of The Black List, a popular website that hosts scripts from screenwriters who were unknowns. Each year, it chooses the top 100 unproduced film scripts and shines a light on the diamonds in the rough that Hollywood rejects. Many of them are discovered, turned into movies, and win tons of awards, including Oscars! In fact, nearly half of the scripts from The Black List have made it to Hollywood and more than 200 of them have won Golden Globes or Academy Awards including *Slumdog Millionaire, Hell, Juno,* and *The King's Speech.* At the time of this writing, The Black List films have earned Hollywood more than $30 billion. Talk about disruptive!

Franklin Leonard had earned his place in the industry and was well-respected and highly connected. I thought that, if The Black List had many scripts to review each year and was employing readers to dig through the endless pile, they might benefit from ScriptBook technology to help them weed through it all. Two birds… one stone. I could get ScriptBook AI the national attention, recognition, and respect it deserved while helping the struggling unknowns fighting for their chance in the industry. Better films would be made displacing the rotten tomatoes taking up space at the box office.

Franklin Leonard took my call. Not only is he a Harvard graduate and one of the smartest people I have ever met, he is also kind and generous. I liked him instantly and felt I was talking to someone who understood data and the logic behind the story data could tell. We had many discussions about potential collaborations, but they came with a stark warning: "Nadira, I know how Hollywood is," he said. "Traditional, conservative. I also know screenwriters. Nitpicky. Complex. Vehemently resistant to both change and criticism." He gave me a new perspective on the personality of a screenwriter. I confessed to him that his characterization of their psyches was different from what I saw in the long lines of people waiting to talk to me at the film festivals. Those people seemed eager, open, and hungry for a shot. How could these be the same types of people?

He assured me that he shared my belief that the future was moving toward AI. And people who have been waiting for a nibble will jump at the first morsel thrown their way. But after a few bites, they would likely drop their guard and reveal that they are fussy and rigid. Franklin Leonard worried that ScriptBook AI might be ahead of its time. He felt the "lights" were off in Hollywood as it related to AI analysis before greenlighting a script. Still, he was willing to be the first to test the power of ScriptBook so his company could be ahead of the curve.

We thought about how to offer a ScriptBook AI report at a low price point and offer it to writers, producers, and filmmakers. Then we got to work developing a four-page report that showcased the most useful data from the outputs we received. And we designed the pdf version report, offered for sale at $99. The price point seemed right since other companies were offering script assessments by humans for $150 or more. Our price was right, and a struggling creative could pay for it.

It was packaged as "The Black List powered by ScriptBook AI." Genius! All that was left was for the lawyers to hammer out the wherefores and hereinafters. Franklin and I were kindred spirits. I understood his mission, and he understood mine. Once the paperwork was done, he offered another word of advice: "Brace yourself. We will have some backlash. But we'll see what comes of it." My team worked around the clock to have the report ready by April of 2017 while The Black List team drafted a press release extolling the power of technology. It said, in part, that although human expertise was a critical component, adding the AI component would enhance the industry. They announced the partnership between ScriptBook AI and The Black List! I couldn't help but scream, "Yes!" when I saw it. My tiny Belgian startup of hardworking people had gotten its foot in the door in a big way. There were pros and cons to this partnership, but Franklin and I discussed them all at length, mitigating any downsides as best we could and maximizing the benefits.

The morning of the official launch was evening in Belgium. So, I went to bed naively thinking it would be several days before we would see any reaction to our press releases and other marketing effort. When I awoke the next morning, my phone was bursting with notifications. Twitter had exploded. Podcasts were abuzz with conversation about us. News reports were airing everywhere. You would have thought Franklin and I discovered a tiny little village of people living on Mars. Actually, you would have thought we *killed* a little tiny village of people living on Mars!

The reaction was shock, fear, and confusion that we would launch AI driven script analysis. We expected a measure of negativity from people who didn't want to accept something new moving into their neighborhood. But the respond was overwhelmingly critical. We could not have predicted this level of backlash. It seemed that everyone with a keyboard had an opinion about what we were doing. I imagined blue-haired grandmothers at retirements homes sipping their meal replacements angrily tapping away at how AI was taking over the world while, at the same time, Armani-clad execs sat in coffee houses in front of laptops berating us for removing the human element from their artform. It seemed the whole film and TV world was against us. Thanks to Reddit threads and Twitter feeds, the conversations survive to this day.

> *"Fear for the day studios begin this type*
> *of computer-based analysis."*

or

"I doubt many writers will find value in this product at $100. Those that do, probably shouldn't be spending it. If you need a machine to tell you what genre you wrote, you've got bigger problems".

or

I don't see any benefit at all to this ScriptBook stuff. I prefer to take Brian Koppelman's advice and "calculate less."

I tried to fend off the storm of negative replies. But that backfired as well. People assumed I was AI responding to the complaints. "I am a lady, not a robot," I cried. But my protests fell on deaf (and dumb) ears. Endless rhetoric about the evil we were perpetrating on the industry. And, caught in the crossfire, was Franklin Leonard. The goodwill he had spent years building through a brilliant idea and a winning personality was starting to slip away with every keystone. They called him terrible names and labeled our venture "disgusting." We were buried in conflict. He tried earnestly to respond to every Tweet, post, and comment. He offered to talk with people about the service and insisted that it was merely an option they could accept or ignore. But that was not enough for people. They wanted their pound of flesh.

The industry turned on Franklin. He had spent years establishing ties with the Writer's Guild of America, Nicholl Screenwriting Fellowship, and a host of schools and universities in the U. S. Talent agencies, Hollywood studios, and Academy Award-winning writers always took his calls. He was a big deal. They were sourcing the Black List to find their next projects. The attacks were vile and relentless. References to McCarthyism, Trump, and dehumanization were rampant in the commentary.

On a personal note (I guess this is all somewhat personal), I was disgusted. For all of Hollywood's talk about supporting outsiders, with all their talk about being woke and relevant, they were quick to bury a Black man and an enterprising woman — honest, hard-working innovators — who were teaming up to create something that was designed to improve the movie industry. It left me with a sick feeling in my stomach like a gut punch. It was professional assault and battery on my company, and Franklin Leonard was collateral damage.

The worst criticisms came from the screenwriters themselves. They were the weakest link in the chain and had been for decades. ScriptBook's mission was aimed at giving them more access, not less. We were the only company at the time who cared enough to make technology like this widely available to the rank and file. Successful podcasts run by screenwriters devoted hours of their broadcasts to discredit. Greg Mazin of *Chernobyl* and *Hangover* fame, John August, writer of *Charlie's Angels* and *Big Fish*, and Brian Koppelman of *Billions* were saying the meanest things. Not one of them invited me on their podcast show or admitted to having heard me speak. I didn't hear any commentary that suggested they had done intensive research on my company. All I heard were accusations about a company they had painted as the big, bad wolf. Another podcaster referred to ScriptBook as a "shady Belgian company" as if we were running drugs, smuggling guns, and crating human beings for the sex trade. And what was our criminal enterprise? AI. It was laughable when it didn't send me running to the bathroom to surrender my lunch as a peace offering to the porcelain god.

I get it! No one wants their work judged by anyone. Script writers hold their breath after they submit a script and wait to hear what an actor, producer, or director thought of it. Every student who submits a term paper or essay knows that feeling. And writers are judged every day. So, it stands to reason that the thought of a computer judging their work without them having the ability to explain various points or argue about the results left a bitter taste in their mouths. So bitter, in fact, they couldn't see past the minor negatives to the glaring positives: ScriptBook would bring to light some of the fabulous scripts that were being overlooked. The AI script analysis would provide actionable feedback to help them write more engaging and potentially more successful scripts. It was a win-win-win-win! But I couldn't lead these horses to water, so I couldn't make them drink. I tugged on their reigns, and they buck-kicked me back to Belgium.

Yes, this was personal. I couldn't watch their movies anymore. I wondered how they could bear the sight of themselves in the mirror. It wasn't enough for them to disagree with our premise that AI could predict the success or failure of a movie or television script. They seemed hell bent on destroying ScriptBook's reputation and painting me as a front for the Belgian mob. I was right back in the STEM school getting my hair pulled and faceplanting when some boy stuck his foot out to trip me. Only this time, I couldn't fight back. My enemies were everywhere. They slithered out from under every rock. They threw rocks at me from every side. The only way to retaliate against them was to be successful.

One producer, Keith Calder of *All the Boys Love Mandy Lane* won the award for most hateful. He admitted that he had never heard of the company or heard me speak before he launched a campaign to destroy ScriptBook. He wrote somewhere around a dozen tweets. I've saved them as screenshots—to remind myself just how vile humans can be. The worst of them was: "*ScriptBook is snake oil garbage masquerading as an objective tool. Writers and executives, please give this a hard pass.*" And those were just

ScriptBook's famous enemies. Plenty of unknowns took to social media to sling mud our way. It was cancel-culture before cancel-culture was cool. This was decidedly *not* cool. It was dishonest and lacked integrity. Had they called me, I would have had a conversation with every one of them. They would have known that I was not mafia or sinister or a shyster. One conversation would have given them a glimpse into my vision and convinced them that I was sincere. Perhaps I wouldn't have been able to convince them of the efficacy of my technology. But I would have at least shown them who I was and nullified any thought that I wasn't a legitimate entrepreneur with a legitimate product. They would have had a balanced view. But there is none so blind as he who will not see.

For all of Hollywood's talk about supporting women's rights, they buried *this* woman for no apparent reason. It wasn't because of reasoned analysis. It wasn't the result of thorough research. There was no hearty debate. It was just hair pulling, eye-scratching, and boys dressed as men sticking their foot out to trip me as I walked by. I was up against the old boys' club, and I was the girl with cooties trying to get into the clubhouse. I was a threat. I was not to be investigated. Surely not validated. I was to be eradicated. They circled the wagons and made sure I didn't have a prayer. The only thing that could save me from the predators was to make ScriptBook AI wildly successful. Then, I would be undeniable.

In 2017, the fierceness of the attacks against ScriptBook were the worst they had ever been. It took mental gymnastics to take myself back to those days when writers stood in line to tell me their tales of woe. *Was I dreaming? No, that really happened.* One person after another came up to me crying (literally and figuratively) about how they needed ScriptBook AI to help them. They just wanted a fair chance. They felt weak and powerless. They complained that no one would listen. They lamented that they had no way to prove that their script was marketable. They needed an edge. ScriptBook provided them that edge. And they turned on the company. I felt foolish. I had fallen for the pitch the writer's sold me. They told me they needed an answer. They moaned about being weary running around California with the same project under their sweaty armpits for years. I changed the scope of our mission to include them and made it our business to keep ScriptBook AI affordable and accessible to all. It had cost millions to build this technology. But we priced it at a paltry $99. I ran to their aid like the townsmen in the *Boy Who Cried Wolf.* The writers claimed they were being eaten alive, abused by Hollywood wolves. Then, when I came running with my pitchfork to rescue them, they became abusers themselves. It would have been a fascinating anthropological or psychological experiment. But I had no time or space to debate the social aspect of what was happening because it was my life. It was livelihood. It was my baby. And it was the jobs of my team — all on the line on this one big bet. *What a stupid cow, I was.*

The only person I felt sorry for was Franklin Leonard. He joined this mission with the same heart and goal to help writers and suffered in the process. But the comments about him and about The Black List continued and even increased in their disturbing tone:

"This is complete and utter garbage. It's telling you stuff about your own script any reasonable person could figure out on their own. If they wanted to offer this as a free "bonus" to their hosting or paid evaluations, that would be one thing. But to charge $100 for a program to analyze your script is insulting and quite honestly, a scam. I'm done supporting Franklin and the Blacklist. This is a

shameless cash grab and offers no value to writers whatsoever."

"Furthermore, this leaves no doubt in my mind that Franklin purposefully intended to deceive writers into thinking that submitting their script to the blacklist website might give them a chance to be on the annual blacklist for the purposes of making more money. That was always something I gave Franklin the benefit of the doubt for before but not anymore.

You lost a supporter today Franklin."

Franklin Leonard responded by offering free analyses to a select number of people to help ease the friction and get some good comments generated. In no time, he had a full roster of writers wanting to use ScriptBook AI. But that did little to calm the vitriol. I knew it wouldn't be long before my phone rang and his deep, gentle voice greeted me on the other hand. One night, that call arrived. Franklin advised me that the call was on speakerphone and his lawyer was sitting next to him. "Franklin," I said softly, "you don't need your lawyer. I'm not your enemy. I understand what you are going through. I have a tender heart, perhaps too tender for this industry. Just tell me what you want to do, and I'll do it. I saw the criticism. I saw the horrible words that were thrown at us." We talked friend to friend. "Nadira, I knew we would have backlash. I warned you it would come. Anything new is met with a dose of rejection. But I had no idea it would be this intense. This is something I did not expect. We have to cancel our agreement. People I have worked with for the past fifteen years who respected and trusted me dropped me within 24 hours of the press release.

Organizations and Guilds are threatening to cut ties with me. Hollywood producers and screenwriters are threatening to boycott my company unless I kill this partnership. I'm sorry."

"I understand. Don't apologize. I completely understand. You spent fifteen years building your brand. It took guts for you to take a chance on me."

The Black List was in critical condition but had a chance to be saved. But ScriptBook … ScriptBook was like a Stage 4 cancer patient. Our prognosis was bleak at best. We were hated, feared, and shunned. They had cut off their noses to punish their faces. Speaking of faces…. I was the face of ScriptBook AI. But the metaverse was content to depersonalize ScriptBook. They had done to me precisely what they claimed to fear I'd do to them: remove the human element. Nobody invited me to the conversation about *me*. It was sufficient to shoot darts at me and hide behind their papers, blogs, and podcasts — never having to face the object of their disdain. They painted ScriptBook AI as a mafia-esque group of felons hiding away in a dark basement developing our sinister plot to take over the movie industry. It was easier to break us from afar than engage me in conversation, understand our work, and criticize it fairly. I was certain ScriptBook could stand up to the scrutiny. But people who were illiterate in the field of data science dismissed us as snake oil salesmen. Come on, people. Step into the light. Strangely enough, everyone knew the age of AI was coming in movies and television. AI is actively involved in matchmaking services, cryptocurrency, and medical services like surgery. How on earth did the entertainment industry expect it would remain a place of hunches, gut feelings, and instinct?

The Black List collaboration was over. Making the announcement to my team was more painful than I imagined when I was practicing my speech to them that we lost The Black

List. We had seen this partnership as legitimization of our work. The looks on the faces of my team depicted the brokenness inside my heart. They were stunned. These lovely, gentle, kind scientists were not ready to be in the ring with the lions, tigers, and bears of the industry. They listened in shock as I detailed how the world we had come to help, had torn us apart. Lifeguards often talk of being assaulted by their victims. As they seek to pull them from the water, the victims struggle so violently, the lifeguards often emerge with broken noses, bruises, and scratches. I may sound self-congratulatory to portray the movie industry as drowning and ScriptBook AI like some Savior. But the data doesn't lie. In 2009, box office gross was 10.6 billion dollars. In 2017, it was 11.07 billion, failing to keep pace with the rate of inflation. And with so many movies losing millions, it sure seemed like a financial tsunami:

- *Cats* lost around 113 million dollars.
- *A Wrinkle in Time* lost over 100 million dollars.
- *Dark Phoenix* lost about 133 million dollars.
- *Mulan* is reported to have lost 140 million dollars.
- Even with Will Smith providing star power, *Gemini Man* lost 111 million dollars.

More than eighty-six percent of movies that are released every year <u>fail</u> to become successful at the box office. Most people are genuinely surprised to learn that. But stats don't lie. Even large production companies often don't earn back the millions of dollars they sink into making most of their movies. When I found out about this strange truth, I wasn't overly surprised. For me, Los Angeles is the true representative of the movie industry where everything appears glamorous, but a lot of damage is going on underneath. That's probably one of the underlying factors for my animosity against L.A. How many investors in these bombs are still scratching their head wishing they could have seen into the future and prevent such a loss. *Voila, idiots! ScriptBook AI!!*

Forget the effects of COVID on the movie industry in 2020 and 2021. The movie industry was suffering from self-inflicted wounds long before the first tiny virus hopped off the airplane, stretched it legs, looked around and started its tour of every city, town, and village in the U. S. To that point, the movie industry's attempt to recover from COVID would have been helped greatly by ScriptBook in a time when movie houses could ill-afford to release junk. People already felt like going to the movies was playing Russian Roulette with their lives. To take the risk and buy a high-ticket price only to have a bad movie experience was something moviegoers loathed. But no one saw ScriptBook AI as the answer. It was just another foe to defeat.

In particular, I felt betrayed by the screenwriters. In Hollywood circles, they are the lowest of the low. No one gives a shit about a screenwriter until they have a hit. They spend thirty years being treated like a zero while other writers who were one-hit wonders continue to be invited to the industry parties and always get a sit down with producers. They transact on that one hit for years while up and coming screenwriters turn into old men and women waiting for their shot. ScriptBook AI promised to end that kind of subjectivity. With a few clicks, hundreds of scripts could be evaluated, allowing the cream to rise to the top regardless of who the writer was. The days after The Black List pulled the plug on us were terrible, and I felt bitterness settling into my heart, further cemented when I read Franklin Leonard's next press release which he titled "Mea Culpa." It read, in part:

Yesterday afternoon we suspended the ability to purchase a ScriptBook report and will be removing the offering from The BlackList website…

We stand by our belief that there is great potential value for writers in ScriptBook's work, especially in the narrowly tailored report we were offering…

But more importantly, it is also our belief — a fundamental one — that a primary reason for our existence is to support the writing community, both professionals and aspiring professionals.

The last 48 hours have made it very clear that an overwhelming majority of the writing community not only believes that the report has little value but that it shouldn't be offered to those who believe it does.

Serving any community means listening to it, especially when there is such full-throated consensus. We've heard you, and the report is no longer available via The BlackList.

We were, are, and will remain an organization that celebrates, reveres, and often stands in awe of writers, and today is no different. No matter how difficult it was to hear some of the feedback about our decision (I will say that "You'd fit in well in the Trump administration" felt unnecessarily hurtful and inaccurate,) we sincerely appreciate it — all of it — if for no other reason than that it allows us to better serve.

I'd also like to extend a personal thank you to Craig Mazin, John August, and Brian Koppelman, all of whom were particularly vocal in expressing their (negative) opinion both privately and publicly but were generous enough to emphasize their past and ongoing support for our other work…

Up until then, I thought I could not be more devastated. However, the press release proved there were deeper depths my heart could sink to. I was wallowing somewhere under the tick on a cow's rear end. Franklin had faced the threat of the loss of his company simply for offering ScriptBook AI. Imagine it. One woman in a tiny company of 12 data scientists, in a tiny city, in a tiny country was the spark of a firestorm felt around the other side of the world. They say all publicity is good publicity. Whoever said that should have seen what happened with ScriptBook in 2017. Why this overreaction? It was like dropping a nuclear bomb on a beehive. Then a revelation…

We had hit a nerve. ScriptBook AI was on the right track. The idea that any one person has his or her finger on the pulse of Hollywood and could pick a winning script was nonsense. Most scripts were cut, chopped, and pumped up so relentlessly that the final version didn't resemble the original at all. Instead, they could have chosen quality scripts from the beginning that had real punch and the ability to draw viewers, which, in turn, meant more money for the studios. If nothing else, I knew I had exposed Hollywood. The sabotage effort was evidence that ScriptBook AI was the real deal. If they truly thought it was useless, it would have died on the vine and would have disappeared like so many other bad ideas. But the onslaught was proof that the bad guys in Hollywood were like gangsters protecting their earnings. You remember the days when a group of thugs would come in and bust up a small shopkeeper's store? As the shopkeeper repaired and rebuilt the store, the thugs returned and offered a warning, "If you don't want this to happen again, you better pay us a percentage of your business every week… forever." That's Hollywood! Hollywood had set up the perfect system to preserve itself: pretend that there was some magic in their picks, demand billions of dollars from moviegoers to keep themselves in the money and then beat to a pulp anyone who sought to expose them or revolutionize the industry.

The social media onslaught did not stop after The Black List pulled out. I called it Hell Weeks because it continued for weeks and weeks afterwards. The "I told you so" chorus took the stage and sang their dissonate songs. There was some positive social media response. But the balance was ninety percent vs. ten percent. So, we didn't stand a chance. Even people from our home region in Europe joined the fray against ScriptBook despite the fact that I was a European business owner. Americans are famous for their brutal frankness. Many deemed me worthy of nothing short of death. But Europeans are, on balance, slower to react and more measured. They could have easily been the voice of reason and provided an opportunity to present the counterpoint. Besides, acceptance in Europe offered extrapolates to adoption in the U. S. But, sadly, no one called from any country. Everyone just typed. Clickity clack went the keys, typing out ScriptBook's doom. Negative voices are so strong in our culture. The loud, blaring voices seem to always win. Reason gets lost in the noise.

THE HUMAN ELEMENT

At this point, it would be fair to briefly "strong man" the opposing view of ScriptBook AI. A strong man argument takes the side of one's opposition. I think I can see what worried my detractors and state their case fairly. Here goes! The primary complaint was the loss of human element. Reducing script analysis to an AI, they said, was a fool's errand because no AI could possibly feel what a human being feels, when they read a script. A machine could never connect on a visceral level with the deep emotions a movie or television show is attempting to elicit. I concede. There is no replacement for humans. None. And the technology does not yet exist, as far as I know, that can interpret data the way humans can. It's been tried on multiple fronts. War games attempt to use AI to determine whether to fire or not in a hostile territory.

But ScriptBook AI was never attempting to replace humans. It was meant to be a tool in the hands of humans to perform their work more efficiently. How many great scripts end up in the trash can because some intern, unable to evaluate the marketability of a script, simply eliminates it? The sheer number of incoming scripts meant that script evaluation was limited to the first three or four pages of a script. If it doesn't dazzle and amazes someone's eyes quickly, it gets chucked. I once asked the executives at one of the biggest talent agencies in Hollywood, we'll call them Famous Actors Agency, how they managed to get through so many scripts. "Oh no," one of the executives said. "The assistants don't read them! They have strict instructions to start at page one and stop at page three!"

I had a business meeting with Jane Austen who not only worked at Famous Actors Agency, but also doubled as one of its partners. Once, in a business conversation with Jane Austen, she revealed to me that the agency received up to eight thousand movie scripts a month. I was astonished. "Eight thousand?" I said, with a gasp. "Oh boy, that's one giant slush pile, one that might be considered insurmountable." Jane Austen gave me a half smile, the corners of her eyes squeezing into small wrinkles behind her thick-rimmed glasses, hinting that she had been in the game a long time. Those little laugh lines and crow's feet were the price she chose to pay for her position in the industry. She had grown accustomed to the work and was so ensconced at this point, she would likely never escape.

I took the opportunity to explain how my product worked, telling her that it took just ten minutes for my AI system to read and analyze a script. I promised that we could help reduce their slush pile effectively and make solid predictions about which scripts to take on as projects that were likely to be profitable. We could use the AI system to analyze eight thousand scripts in just two or three days, depending on compute power. If Jane Austen was surprised by my proclamations, she did not show it. She just stared at me from behind her glasses. I took her silence as a cue to continue. I informed her that our AI recognized both a movie's propensity for critical as well as commercial success. With our built-in search system, the agency would be able to source through thousands of analyzed projects and filter them according to audience demographics, lead gender, topic, or themes. We could effectively offer then a stack of movie scripts that passed the profitability threshold and they could choose from there. Still, nothing but silence. I went on and told her that our system had features that could pigeonhole blockbuster movie scripts separate from independent creative movies. The AI worked in a way that didn't marginalize any type of movie script.

Finally, she spoke just as I was thinking I should rush over to the case on the wall and fire up the defibrillator! We came down to an agreement. ScriptBook AI would do the script analysis and Famous Actors Agency would make the final decisions. *Perfect! That is how it should be!* During the process, anything that had to be automated would simply be run through our system. She was happy to relieve their junior agents from the task of reading through the first couple of pages of eight thousand scripts. "You know," she confessed. "The agents do not read the scripts anyway. Our junior agents or interns do. We give the junior agents and interns the task of reading the scripts with a strict instruction not to read beyond a few pages." This was the second time a senior executive was confessing to this disturbing fact. I was shocked that she said it aloud.

It was such a brutal, uncanny procedure that left me feeling sorry for writers who had poured their hearts and souls into their work, hoping someone would acknowledge their talent. As I learned firsthand how these agencies operate, I couldn't help but wonder how hard it might be for writers to get a breakthrough. Perhaps, my situation was not too different from some of these writers. We were both trying to sell our own form of innovation, creativity, and intellectual property. It was another case of passion wasted on a condescending industry where a person's best efforts were thwarted by a deeply flawed and archaic system. Just imagine… Not a single agent reads the works that writers submit to the agency, and yet they call themselves talent agents. How can they expect to discover unique talents if they never engage with the talented? In Hollywood, things seemed to be purposefully turned upside down. Nothing is ever linear or logical; it was all luck and cutting corners. No story can be fairly evaluated in its first three pages or even its first ten pages, when the story has barely started. Even though I wasn't an expert in scriptwriting, I thought I could have done a better job if I was a talent agent. And the poor writers! It simply meant that as a writer, you are substandard by the judgement of an intern who cannot write better than you. What a pathetic irony!

As if this ugly tale could not get any uglier, these maltreated scripts end up dumped and forgotten. Once, I walked into an office for a meeting at a film production company and saw a pile of scripts used as support to balance a table. Dismal! The writers place their trust — their careers — in the hands of these talent agencies, and they respond by essentially spitting on their hard work and dreams. And how many great writers have given up because they assume that an industry expert, an agent, has rejected their submissions. If only these writers could see how their work was treated, they'd burst into tears. These agents were only interested in submissions from friends, big and powerful names, or others in their network. It is nepotism at its finest — or at its worst. The rest are doomed for the trash can at worst or a table leg at best.

I felt disheartened about the whole thing and had to speak up. "Look," I said. "I think what you guys are doing is unfair. I am shocked that this is your system. Please use my AI so that you are able to give a fair chance to each writer who is looking to have the agency read his or her script." That is why I love science and technology. It's fair! The AI doesn't give a damn whether the script was written by an influential person or famous performer or a waiter in a restaurant. It doesn't care if the writer is White or Black or Asian or Arab or any other label in society. I kept going back and forth with Famous Actors Agency over that, and I had some of the executives in support of me, and as it turned out, some were against me because they did not want the system that could bring radical change. At the end, the deal with Jane Austen at Famous Artists Agency fell through. I can't say I was surprised.

One morning at an early meeting with Famous Artists Agency, the executives showed up and offered some cock and bull story that even a child would find hard to believe. They claimed that my proposal would burden them with the task of contacting every writer for permission to allow the AI to read their scripts. They said they could not do that because it was impossible for them to run after each writer for permission considering their limited time and resources. Bullshit! I had four of the executives on my side including Jane Austen, who wanted to go through with the AI program. She spoke out in the meeting quite boldly. "We need this AI program in our agency." But the top brass of the agency was not to be swayed. Interestingly, a few weeks after the meeting, I ran into Jane Austen at Toronto film festival, and she outright told me that even if ten of the executives agreed to a proposal, if the company chiefs voted against it, it was dead. There and then, I saw the extent to which dictatorship was deeply entrenched in the system. Egos were the cog in the wheels of progress. The ugliness of the system was insufferable.

How deluded people are to think, from the outside looking in, that Hollywood is the greatest entertainment vehicle in the world. How wrong they are! ScriptBook AI offered them a solution that promised to improve their work and make them money. But they were so blinded by their titles, positions, offices, and status, they couldn't see it. ScriptBook could look at the script in its totality and determine whether the data points and parameters that made movies successful were present. Then the script would be flagged and forwarded to the human who could read through it to try to verify what the AI concluded.

All in all, it was a fairer treatment of the script than it could have gotten otherwise. At the time of this writing, nothing has noticeably changed for those struggling writers who trashed ScriptBook AI. They are still knocking on the same doors that remained closed to them years ago. They are still sweaty and desperate, praying for someone to give them their due, open the opportunities for them. They are still visualizing in their meditation times that they will get their big chance, and their fabulous script will make it past the intern who split his or her time between reading scripts and checking their Instagram. Did they replace ScriptBook AI with something better? No. I continued to be invited to speak at conferences and film festivals. I dutifully boarded the plane, booked my hotel, and showed up in my power suit to give my presentation. I answered the Q&As with the same passion and confidence — perhaps more. But when the line formed at the foot of the stairs leading down from the stage, I offered a polite wave and declined to chat, citing a busy schedule as my reason. The real reason: the bitter taste left in my mouth by the screenwriters. I had no interest in listening to them boo-hoo about their sad struggles when I held them responsible for their own pain. It is one thing to backseat drive and complain about every turn the driver makes. It's another thing to be offered the driver's seat and refuse to sit down. They might have had an opportunity to see on paper that their script had been evaluated and the outcome mapped out in the data points reached. They might have had a concrete way to demonstrate the potential financial viability of their movie script through a ScriptBook report. But, as a group, they passed. So, I passed them.

I attended a high-profile entertainment and tech convention where various movie studio executives were in attendance. As I sat in the large hall, which was flooded with lights, I couldn't stop wondering how pathetic the charade was that I witnessed. Executives in their well-tailored suits gaily shook hands and smiled at each other, seemingly happy to see each other. I gazed at them as they walked in and sat down. As the conference started, they appeared to listen to a dark-haired middle-aged man with a bare forehead and eyes that enthusiastically expressed conviction as he gave his speech. The keynote speaker then addressed the audience, talking to us about the potential of technology in the entertainment industry. I could confirm some of the points the speaker made in his speech. I also learned quite a bit, since I brought an open mind to these events. But I can't say the same for the entertainment executives who were in attendance. After the one-hour address, I walked up to meet the speaker, Bob Scholes, a futurist for Platform Studios, another major Hollywood film studio.

I introduced myself as the CEO of ScriptBook AI and explained what we did. He listened attentively to me, his grey eyes roving around my face as he nodded at what I was saying. Then I asked him why the film industry had refused to incorporate the use of AI tools to help inform whether a movie would be successful or not. Bob rolled his eyes and straightaway told me to stop being so naive. That was not the response I was expecting. He pointed out to me that the industry was banal and that any form of improvement or innovation was fiercely resisted. The industry was a giant stereotype. I watched the red hues of hatred and helpless rage grow in his eyes. He told me that the studio where he worked would prefer to continue to use typewriters if they could get away with it. The irony was that they bothered to employ him as their futurist to help spread the gospel of inventive technology. In reality, his position was little more than a façade — a gimmick. "I am a gimmick, a figure-head," he said to me with a shake of the head, a smirk fading out of the corners of his mouth. I saw the pains of maintaining this deceit hidden in the shadows of his eyes as he stared at me. He went on to tell me that he was hired to be a futurist because his employers wanted to be on the frontier of leading technology along the terrain of the entertainment industry or, at least, they wanted to create the impression that they supported technological innovations in the industry. They hired him to feed that illusion. Every other film studio had a futurist within its corridors.

It was a truly eye-opening moment. For half a year, we had been deep into a proof-of-concept with Platform Studios, but this made everything hit home. "So what about ScriptBook's ongoing trial with Platform Studios?" I asked him, finally finding my voice. He told me, without mincing words, that there was probably an executive waiting in the office to say no to my work. I was so stunned by his straightforward answer that my spirit drained out of me and waves of depression swept over me. I felt cheated by the system. I felt as though I was being pushed off to the sidelines like an unwanted specimen. "What advice can you give me on how to get them to accept my technology?" He looked at me quizzically as though I was trying to trick him into confessing to a crime. "Beat the entire industry at their own game. Open your own studio. Seek out writers or producers for the scripts your AI identifies as the best. You'll make a crap load of money and get your revenge against the machine." I was shocked at his advice. On one hand, it would be great to be independent and ensure great movies get made. On the other hand, I knew nothing about making movies and didn't have the gazillion dollars it would take to start my own studio. Still, I fantasized about how it would feel to not be barricaded by any policy. Everything would be mine and I would not have to run to anybody to sign off on a decision or risk them objecting to it. I immediately saw the impossibility of floating Bob's idea. But it was the best idea that anyone could have given me, no matter how unfeasible considering my situation. The bad guys win again.

After the Black List fiasco, I turned inwards. I think most people tend to close their circle when they feel under threat. I was like a wounded deer that drags itself off the highway and found a quiet place in the woods to die. I had been deeply betrayed and terribly hurt. It was hard to know who to trust. I wondered if I could serve this industry at all. ScriptBook AI remained in the eye of the hurricane for at least a couple of months after the Black List collaboration disintegrated. Though the attacks were not as frequent, they were just as intense as ever. The social media posts continued. We saw them. We just decided not to respond. We chose the high road rather than rolling around in the mud with our detractors. But we kept our heads held high and did not engage in the social media massacre. We kept our eyes on the prize: the work, the research, the clients. My team and I were already committed to excellent in terms of the quality of the AI script analysis. But now we were playing catch up on the public relations front. We had to deliver something that was a hair beyond excellent. People were waiting for us to fail, so what we released had to blow their minds.

Despite the backlash, as 2017 turned into 2018, we were extremely productive in terms of software development. We also celebrated a milestone, securing our first commercial contracts with several film funds. On top of that, we closed a deal with a film festival, which planned to use our AI system to evaluate all its film submissions. I had many trips scheduled to either participate on a panel or to deliver the keynote address. But the trips had lost their luster for me. I disliked the atmosphere. I felt the purpose behind the events was no longer clear. I certainly wasn't interested in meeting any disingenuous writers who would cry to me about their stalled careers.

I had lost my passion for speaking. I could no longer see the point. Despite my telling them what ScriptBook AI was and why the time had come for the integration of AI in script analysis and that people needed to open their eyes, nothing I said was helping them do that. I had facts, studies, statistics. None of it seemed to matter. For those ignorant of AI, I was only arousing curiosity. For those knowledgeable about it, I was heightening their fear of the inevitable. I was the embodiment of their dread — that someone would find a way to replace them with a computer. I honored all the commitments I had made for talks and panel discussions, but I refused to book any more. I had some high-profile events scheduled. I couldn't shirk my responsibility. One of the events, in particular, stood out: a high-profile tech and entertainment summit in Silicon Valley, where some of the world's most influential VCs and Hollywood power players would be in attendance and speaking. The founder of YouTube, Steve Chen, was doing one of the talks as well as Patrick Lee, founder of Rotten Tomatoes. At that summit Patrick Lee from Rotten Tomatoes gave me some important insights on the movie business. He told me I still had a rough ride ahead of me and talked about the backlash he encountered when he started Rotten Tomatoes. He said it wasn't even AI giving out scores at that time and still movie executives everywhere were rejecting it. It seems people from the movie business are allergic to any form of criticism.

I stood in the back and watched the crowd at this high-profile event. The room was filled with industry executives, sitting on the edge of the chairs, listening to what each speaker had to say. They had come to the conference to hear about the latest developments in their field. More importantly, they were there to learn about future innovations. But I wondered how many of them were truly open to knowing how technology could help them do their work better. Were they truly willing to accept it? I think not!

Technology is welcomed from production stage to post-release stage. CGI, special effects, even technology that ages actors up or down (see *The Irish Man*) is permitted and relied upon to do what makeup and prosthetics cannot. In *Top Gun: Maverick*, Val Kilmer's voice was replicated using AI technology because Val Kilmer had lost his voice due to throat cancer. Technology that detects audience tastes, marketability, advertising etc. are an easy sell to Hollywood. But, if you do your homework and research on what technologies are being used in the script stage, pre-development, greenlighting, you'll find none. Tech used in these early stages exposes executives as little more than fortune tellers. Without technology exposing their arbitrary greenlight decisions, there is no accountability. Basically, they are keeping AI out of the early stages of the film production chain to protect their jobs. As a result, technology that impacts the early stages of the filmmaking process meets intense resistance. Hollywood folks like having their thumb on the greenlight button. No one else should have the power to approve a film project but those who had earned their place in the upper echelon. As a result, they suffer, and some amazing projects never make it past the front door. One of Hollywood's favorite quotes was uttered by Hollywood screenwriter, William Goldberg, in 1983: "Nobody knows anything." Nobody felt obligated to justify their greenlighting decisions. They just keep consulting the stars, reading crystal balls, and looking at tea leaves. How true! I dutifully gave my remarks with all the passion I could muster. After all, this was my heart and soul. I believe in ScriptBook AI so deeply, it was in my DNA. I bled it. Sweated it. Cried little digital tears. So, I could not dampen my enthusiasm for it in the slightest. And the message did not fall on deaf ears completely.

In 2018, I received a merger offer followed by another. One was a company that was well established for a decade. Its CEO was a knowledgeable man who appears to get the basic of ScriptBook's mission. He had wide experience in the film industry as a producer, financier, and generally as an entrepreneur. He recommended the merger because he felt he could make inroads for ScriptBook AI. He had studied the competition and isolated their weaknesses. His plan for how ScriptBook AI could capitalize on those gaps in the market was very appealing to me. He spoke straightforwardly… something I appreciated after all the lip service I had received from others. "You have the best technology," he said. "It is unmatched. You have a strong product. Your competition is not doing half of what you are able to do." He went on to list some solid reasons for me to consider the merger.

We were not just technology architects; we had teased out the data science that drove the technology and added real value. But we didn't know how to sell it. After our disastrous rollout with the Black List, it was clear we needed help in marketing ScriptBook AI in a way that would increase its chances for adoption. This man's track record in Hollywood was strong. He could, it seemed, get us in front of the right people who could make the decision to implement AI script analysis in their system of evaluating film projects. I must admit, getting the inside track to his network left me salivating. But the relationship, as he laid it out, was reciprocal. By partnering, he felt both his company and mine could dominate the film industry and soon, become the standard for AI script analysis. ScriptBook would become a household name. I was thrilled at the possibility! But… My history with partners, co-founders, collaborators, etc. had been terrible. I was more than a little shell-shocked by it. I pondered the possibility but could not pull the trigger. Looking back, it seems clear that my naivete and trauma from prior experience caused me to reject his offer. It would have been a genius move. It might have changed the game completely for us and could have put us in a different place today. But I was foolish. I wanted to do it on my own. I wanted to break up the all-boys network. I had founded the company, labored over it day and night for years, and brought it this far. I wanted to see it through alone. Mergers, as far as I was concerned, were something to be considered in the next phase of ScriptBook AI, after it had become accepted and adopted in Hollywood. It was too soon, I thought, to be thinking about a merger.

Looking back, I wish I had said yes to the merger. It begs the question: if you are merging at the wrong time, is it better to merge too early, or too late. And the answer is clear. Too late is simply too late. It was one of the biggest mistakes I made in my entrepreneurship journey. Remember, we had turned inwards. We were smarting from our very public failure and feeling the bitterness and resentment from the rejection we received at the hands (and computer keyboards) of the screenwriters. People were still talking about The Black List. To add insult to injury, I started getting press requests about the the Black List fiasco. No one wanted to interview me before publishing the negative stories that killed our collaboration. But once it was dead, everyone wanted to do a post-mortem. Suddenly, I was a human-interest story. They wanted a salacious tale to tell. They wanted clickbait titles to drive their engagement. But I saw it all as negative press — self serving of them to say the least. I would not oblige a single reporter with an interview.

Turning inwards had clear advantages and disadvantages. One advantage was that we could put our heads down, our butts up, and dive deep into the work. I couldn't have been prouder of what our team produced and the ways in which we were able to elevate the technology, data analysis, pattern recognition, and all the other facets of ScriptBook AI that made it stellar. Our development game was A-plus and it led us to the filing of our first patent for the technology. It was intoxicating to see my name on the patent paperwork as an inventor. I had reconciled the dreams of that little girl in the STEM school who knew she was different. All my ambitions coalesced in that moment because I was no less an inventor than any man who had come before me. And I had paved the way for many little girls who would come after me. If they were ever discouraged, they could point to my work and believe that, at the very least, they could create something that never existed in the world before. That is the gift of the inventor… and the gift to the inventor. She gives the world something no one else has made. But she receives as much as she gives. She receives the promise that had been made to her when she was in pigtails and horn-rimmed glasses. "You can be anything you want to be," the world shouts. But the shout is followed by a whisper that says, "In order to get it, you will have to bleed for it."

As I looked back, before the PR - disaster, there was so much to be proud of. I had gotten farther than many women like me had. I had raised the bar and proven what was possible. Looking inward allowed me to consider the wins we had experienced. But the disadvantage of turning inward is that our mindset isn't open to what was being presented to us. Opportunities looked threats. Threats looked like opportunities. This generated a kind of entrepreneurial paranoia that permeated our work throughout 2018. We kept our toys to ourselves rather than being wide open to sharing them with the world. Once bitten, twice shy.

THE UNKINDEST CUT

The leaps we made in technological development might not have been possible if I was still globe-trotting, speaking at industry events. I knew that we had the state-of-the-art technology in AI driven script analysis. It was exceptionally accurate, bulletproof, and the best available anywhere in the world. I had developed a confidence I did not know was possible a few years earlier. When we started, I saw myself as one lone woman in a sea of sharks. I did not trust my instincts or know my potential. But my experiences had forced me to evolve into a mean, lean, project-managing machine. The fear was gone. What remained was steely-eyed determination and an unshakeable faith in what ScriptBook AI could do.

The AI system was completely automated. It would serve the humans well who used it by helping to forecast the potential success of a film script. It had been tested again and again, accurately calling the balls and strikes of existing film projects. Now, all we needed were big clients. We had already signed our first customers, but we needed the big guns who could pay more than six figure deals. I was invited to a gathering of tech executives who were building technology for the financial sector. It was a dinner followed by a movie premiere sponsored by our common investor,

Joe Gazillionaire. All the leaders of the companies he invested in were expected to be there. I showed up thirty minutes late partly because I couldn't find parking and partly because I needed extra time to swallow the bile that was building in my gut. I didn't know what was in store for me that night. But I was sure of one thing. I expected that I would be the only woman present. Again! Sure enough, I walked in and was escorted by the hostess to the dinner table amidst triceps and biceps in their suits and cologne. The bile started inching its way up again. I grabbed a diet coke and tried to wash it back to the pit of my stomach. I greeted everyone and was introduced to the other guests by Joe Gazillionaire.

There were lawyers, entrepreneurs, and friends of his sitting around the long table. I was surprised to see mostly older men and younger women. I wondered who those women might be. A bright spot of hope shined in the darkness of my bitter heart. I was so intrigued about these women and looked forward to swapping stories and tips with them. It was the first time I had a chance to talk to people just like me who were running startup companies. I needed intel! I wanted to hear what their experiences had been and if there was a difference in their experience. I wanted to know if the million dollars I had been given by Joe Gazillionaire was heavier than the millions given to my male counterparts. I started with the women. I made a beeline for a fit young woman and asked about her business. She informed me that she was the date of one of the 60-year-old men. Oh no, there's that bile again. She explained that coming to events like this as arm candy to older men was the only way she had found to get her foot in the door to investors who might someday back her bodybuilding business. "If I want to become a champion in my business, I have to date that prick sitting next to you."

My jaw fell open in an audible gasp. I couldn't believe she had said it out loud. No reservation. No fear that he would hear her. Her cards were on the table and he was the joker. It was clear that she disliked this man and knew she was performing a kind of entrepreneurial escort service. Also clear was his knowledge that he was nothing more than a sugar daddy, there to foot the bill and gain the envious stares of the other jokers. She must have seen the shock on my face because she announced, "I don't care if he hears me." "Why did you come with him if you don't like him?"
"I just need him if I am going to advance my business."

It turned out that all the beautiful twenty-something year old women at the table were dates of the older men. "They are disgusting pigs," my new friend went on to say. I admired her honesty. Because I was late to the dinner, everyone else had ordered their meal and I couldn't order. The waiter offered me a drink as I looked over the menu. "No! No dinner!" Joe Gazillionaire shouted from across this long table. "There is not going to be any ordering dinner. The kitchen closed twenty minutes ago. No ordering dinner now." I wondered why, then, was the waiter offering to take my order. By this point, my heart (and my stomach) were doing somersaults. It seemed to be his goal to deliberately humiliate me in front of everyone by barking "no ordering dinner now" three times. I felt like a poor immigrant begging for food. It hit a nerve with me as such a thing would with any minority in a room filled with people who looked different and had vastly different backgrounds. It flipped my trigger in all the worst ways and I sat there, painfully watching everyone enjoying delicious food, conversations, and laughter. I was again left out. Not one person took a stand in my defense. Of course not. They were all sucking from the riches of Joe Gazillionaire's teat. The sense of not belonging threw me back to a time when being outcast was my identity. All the words confirming how different I was swirled around in my head: immigrant, minority, woman. But I did my best to dismiss the slight. "Do you mind if I order another diet coke," I asked, my voice dripping with sarcasm. "Sure, you can have a soda," Joe barked. *Thanks Dad!*

All eyes were on me, and I could feel the heat rising up my chest and onto my neck. Then it was my turn to watch everyone as they ate their gourmet meals. There I was sipping my little glass of diet coke. A man sitting next to me was kind enough to engage me in conversation. We told each other about our respective businesses. I asked how he found Joe Gazillionaire as an investor. "He is the best investor I could have asked for," the man said. "He has already poured fifteen million dollars into my company. And we have had to pivot a few times because we can't find a business model that works. We haven't made any sustainable revenue yet. But Joe is patient. He is working with me. I was nervous about the problems we have been having with our sales pipeline. But Joe assured me he never gives up on a company he invests in."

I could not believe my lying ears. No way could this man have received more than ten times as much as I did and produced a tenth of what I had. I felt like Alice in Wonderland and the rabbit hole was sucking me in. I had done what the Mad Hatter advised: "It takes all the running you can do, to keep in the same place. If you want to get somewhere else, you must run at least twice as fast as that!" I worked harder, longer, and faster than this man. I had proven results. I had produced more. But I was still less… less… less… I walked up to another man and asked his story. He told me that, after six or seven years, he was loyal to Joe Gazillionaire because Joe continued to support his shitty product. His words… not mine.

After their dinner, they walked from the restaurant to the theater across the street where the movie premiere was taking place. They were all smiles with their millions in the bank and their full bellies while I sat there hurtling toward a zero balance and a belly so empty I worried that the growling might be heard above the movie soundtrack. I briefly considered scavenging untouched food on the plates. But I dutifully followed behind them to the theatre. The red carpet stretched out from the entrance to the theatre and the pop, pop, pop of the cameras blinded our eyes. The staff slipped a VIP bracelet on my thin wrist. I hid in the back and waited for everyone to go in. As the lights dimmed inside, I turned and left. I drove home after stopping for a gourmet Big Mac. The dinner of champions… and frustrated startup CEOs.

Finally, we started getting bigger orders to analyze film scripts and the AI system ran completely autonomously. Day and night, customers would upload their scripts, and the system went to work evaluating the storyline, characters, genre, and marketability of the movie. The algorithm made its predictions and gave actionable intel about where the deficiencies were in the script. And it did it all while the customer was sleeping. I was overjoyed. The panel talks and keynotes were no longer a major part of our marketing strategy. The industry was not open and had made that clear. The current situation was working for them. Interestingly, when I did those industry events and asked about my speaker's fee, I was told by the organizers that they were not offering speakers any renumeration for appearing at their conferences and festivals. I accepted that, happy to just have the free publicity and the opportunity to talk about ScriptBook AI. They offered to cover travel costs and lodging. I saw that as a fair tradeoff for what I expected would be good press. But in true Hollywood form, there was a double-cross. I later learned that every male speaker on the panels with me had been paid. All the keynote speakers — male, of course — had been compensated in addition to their travel expenses.

The bias against women was deep and wide in the industry and showed no signs of budging. There was no conscience. No integrity. No honor. Nepotism, sexism, and misogyny reigned supreme. I was no less a contributor to the events I spoke at than were my male counterparts. Perhaps I didn't have their fame and track record. But they didn't have my genius product either. Besides, I had been invited by these venues to speak. I had not come to them with cap in hand asking for a few minutes on the dais. I was an invited guest. That's a hell of way to treat a guest. Not only had they lied to me outrightly, they also disrespected the time it took to prepare for the event, my travel time, and my time away from my company. And other speakers told me they had traveled first class. Me? Economy. What did Shakespeare call it? "The unkindest cut." It bears repeating that this is supposed to be the most forward-thinking industry, one that sets the pace for race and gender relations in the U. S. and around the world. Hollywood has set itself up as the moral authority. But when it came time for it to live by its own principles, it fell woefully short.

I am reminded of the line spoken by the monsignor in *Guess Who's Coming to Dinner* as he stands beside film legend, Spencer Tracy. Tracy's character, a newspaper magnate, has just learned that his very white daughter is set to marry a Black man. After years and years of writing and fighting on the issue of race equality, he crumbles when the issues lands on his doorstep in real time. The monsignor chuckles:

> *"Rather amusing, too, to see a broken-down old phony liberal come face-to-face with his principles. Of course, I have always believed that in that fighting liberal façade, there must be some sort of reactionary bigot trying to get out."*

That's Hollywood in a nutshell. Publicly liberal. Privately sexist. Publicly forward-thinking. Privately stone-aged. Publicly virtue signaling. Privately protective of male-dominated wealth and power. It makes all its messages about inclusivity as hollow as steel drum, and all the tears shed for the minorities, women, and other excluded classes as plastic as a showroom dummy. They didn't want to see a woman succeed. They just needed to appear to. Hollywood has been playing the long-game. And they have gotten away with it too, because we love our movies and movie stars. We love a great story. We risk $50 in ticket money and another $50 in popcorn and soda to take our little families to the theater to get a glimpse of a world wrapped in tinsel and fortune. It is as close as we will come to the actresses and actors who make us laugh, cry, and feel. But behind the moving picture is a bureaucracy that stands as the gatekeeper. They lock the movie experience behind a big gate and grant access with the hauteur of a French king.

They've got what we want — the movie experience. And they make us pay in every way possible. Like an abused spouse, we return to our abuser again and again. We never call them on their crap because we fear losing what they provide — those ninety minutes that take us away to another world. I get it. I just don't like it. It's a painful reality that people who talk about changing the world really are talking about the changes *you* should make. They are not willing to change anything about their own lives. Just like the 1,500 private jets that brought climate change pundits to the conference on environmental changes, people in power never consider how they violate their own principles. The monsignor was right. Broken-down phonies. Reactionary bigots.

The industry couldn't even drop its bias to pay one female speaker at one of its conferences and fly her there in the same manner as they had all the men. The industry had delivered the same message to me as the boys at the STEM school: "You don't belong here. You are not one of us. We will tolerate you. But we will never validate you."

In the end, it didn't matter. My message was falling on deaf ears. My pearls were landing among swine. My bread was scattered among the dogs. And other biblical metaphors. Was it the message or the messenger? That is the question that remained after all the dust settled. If I had contacted central casting and requested a Matthew-McConaughey knock-off to pose as the face of

ScriptBook AI, would they have been more open? I could have put an earpiece in his ear, stood in the stairwell at the conferences and fed him his lines. He would have smiled his million-dollar smile, pressed the flesh, and offered the twinkle in his eyes as proof of his sincerity. Would they have eaten him up like Christmas cookies? Was my femaleness just too much for them to bear?

2018 was the end of the charade for me. It should have been the high point of my life. Berlin, Toronto, Cannes, Zurich, Karlovy Vary, Sarajevo, Venice, Hollywood. In any other situation, this would have been a bucket list year. Sarajevo film festival was particularly disappointing. It was a magical place I had always wanted to visit. But I was there to put myself in front of the firing squad yet again. I remember sitting in a packed conference room beside my CTO waiting to be called up to do our dual-presentation. We were slated to share the technology and offer a demo to show how it worked. Then… the Q&A. People sometimes asked questions for which there was no answer. Often, they were barely questions. A woman stood and introduced herself as a creative writing professor at UCLA. Upon hearing that, my anxiety for Q&A subsided and I was anxious to hear her question. But she went on the attack, berating me for stripping the creative writing process and threatening the demise of screenwriters everywhere. "How can you sleep at night," she asked, "knowing that you have singlehandedly destroyed the screenwriting industry, killed creativity, and robbed good, hardworking people of their jobs." Wow! I was stunned by the question. She clearly had not listened to my presentation. I suspect she had stepped off the plane with her guns so loaded, she should've been stopped by airport security. She was angry and confrontational. She didn't want answers. She wanted my head.

I wanted to tell her to give me her iPhone, let me throw it in an incinerator, and have her pledge to never buy one again. Only that would prove that her own actions were consistent with her criticism of me and ScriptBook AI. But I knew the truth (and so did she) that she would sooner run over her grandmother with a Mack truck than give up her iPhone. Yet it was filled with apps that did things for her she once had to hire a human to do. Ignorant woman! I wanted to tell her that she got to the conference with the help of AI. AI booked her flight, gave her directions to the conference center, suggested her hotel, and would likely give her recommendations for where to eat her dinner. But she had the nerve to suggest that AI could not evaluate words in a script and determine whether they might make a viable film? She had no issue with AI helping with her accounting, choosing men for her to date, administering her investments, mining her bitcoins, and driving her car. But flipping through the pages of the script and returning data about it was akin to the antichrist?? I kept my cool, though I have some faint memory of blanking out and accusing her of being allergic to AI.

When I got back on the airplane after the conference was over, steam was still rising from my hair. Furious only scratches the scratch on the surface. I declared, "No more festivals and conferences." No sooner had the words escaped my lips did I remember I was already booked for Venice International Film Festival in a few weeks. I wanted to stomp and scream, "No!" But I knew I had to go in just once more to face the music. How bad could it be? Famous last words.

The Venice Film Festival had different types of presentations featured in it which included keynote speeches, pep talks and panel discussions. I was invited to be one of the keynote speakers for the event. Quite unexpectedly, the moment I arrived in Venice, I was treated like a princess. A car was waiting for me at the airport, and I was immediately lodged in one of their finest hotels. To my pleasant surprise, I had a personal valet assigned to me. At the right moments, she handed me my robe, put my slippers by the bed, and placed chocolate on my bed while asking me if I wanted my bathing water hot or warm. It was one of the most mesmerizing, OMG moments in my life. I felt like I had died and gone to heaven to be served by the angels. It was hardly real. That moment defined being successful as far as materialism was concerned. There were several SVPs and CEOs at the Venice Film Festival and, notably, Big Star Agency.

Big Star Agency was a high-profile outfit that only represented Hollywood's biggest stars. It was run by four managing partners, one of whom I tried to approach, George Wickham. George Wickham came from Hollywood royalty. His mother was an Oscar winning actress and his wife was an Oscar winning screenwriter. I thought I had finally gotten the chance to meet George Wickham in person and to speak to him about ScriptBook AI. I decided to approach him — not immediately, but when a more natural window presented itself. That happened the following day. I was walking down the hallway the next day when I encountered George Wickham at close quarters. He was sitting on a couch in the lobby, deep in conversation perhaps with one of his friends. Although I found it a bit tricky to tell whether the said friend was a human or a doll. Every part of his face had undergone quite a few plastic surgeries so now he couldn't have looked any more synthetic. Almost like a character from a video game. Was he Freddie Kruger sitting there big as life in a fancy Italian lobby? Probably so, since I couldn't bring myself to look at him. I angled my gaze to George Wickham and introduced myself and ScriptBook to him.

I asked if it was possible for us to schedule a meeting for the following day so we could sit and discuss Scriptbook's AI. But George Wickham muttered that planning a schedule for the following day wasn't an option because he had to care for his aging mother who needed nursing. But I knew it was all cock and bull story. He could have just looked me in the eye and turned down the request. I would have been fine with it without even batting an eyelid. But he preferred to cook up a story of an ailing mother just to get rid of me even though I knew very well that his mother was going to receive a lifetime achievement award at the festival the following day. He suggested we could meet the day after. I had no other choice than to agree with the hope he'd honor his word. Although I had gotten a meeting scheduled with him, I couldn't help but notice that his character was very demeaning, especially for someone who had gained a high level of respect in the industry. He was a sharp contrast to the friendly guy who spoke on the festival stage. The following day, which was Saturday, I got into a group photoshoot with the other speakers at the event, CEOs of powerful Hollywood companies such as Famous Actors Agency, Yonis Studios, Platform Pictures, Big Star Agency, and George Wickham. They were all men. I was the only woman present. The photographer insisted that I come forward and stand in the front row. I was in the midst of Hollywood's most powerful and influential people.

Each time George Wickham and I locked gazes, he always averted his eyes sharply like he was sick of seeing me. *Jeez man, get a grip! It's not like I'm going to come after you like a serial killer.* I didn't quite understand why he was actively dodging me. On Sunday, which was the day slated for charitable activities, I was playing tennis. I was crap at it. I tried to get George Wickham to speak to me but gave up because I got the impression that he didn't want to talk. I decided I was going to let him be and find another time to speak to him. After the Venice Film Festival was over, I decided to email him and request to schedule a meeting when I was in Los Angeles next time. I wrote to him and requested an audience, informing him that I would be in L.A. soon. He obliged and hinted his eagerness to see how our AI system worked. George Wickham referred me to his assistant to schedule time and date.

A few weeks later I travelled to L.A. for my scheduled business meetings, among them George Wickham from Big Star Agency. By the time I walked into Big Star Agency 's building complex, I was swept off my feet by the great sights. It was so big and polished with its high-ceilings beset by dazzling glass. People walked in all directions, looking business-like, and seeming to have a place where they urgently needed to be at that precise moment. They had their headphones on, tapping their fingers on the telephones or computers as they talked to whoever was at the other end of the line. I thought I had stepped onto the set of *The Devil Wears Prada*. Except no one was acting. This was their real work environment. I was shocked to learn that women in these places actually walk around in expensive clothes and high heeled shoes, click-clacking against marble floors and makeup so thick, they looked like Kabuki performers. Everyone was an actor with a slash after their job titles: receptionist – slash – actress, security guard – slash – actor, janitor – slash – actor. And the women were so pencil thin, I had to suppress the urge to feed them. The look on their faces when they saw Plain Jane me, was the look you get when you discover some furry food that got lost in the back of the refrigerator. I told one of the model-like receptionists that I was there to meet with George Wickham. They all looked at me in such stunned silence, I felt I should reassure them. "Really," I said. "I have an appointment." Some other executives came to meet me — not George Wickham, who I was there to see. I looked them over. They were so young they couldn't have legally ordered a single glass of wine between them. "I am so sorry. But he is not going to be able to see you today," one of the baby faces said. "What?" I answered. "I fly in all the way from Belgium, and he can't honor our appointment? You are kidding, right?"

I was a visitor paying him a visit in his empire, it was kind of rude for him to ghost me that way, and after all, I had other important meetings to attend to that day. If I knew he wouldn't be attending the meeting, I definitely wouldn't have bothered coming. I was infuriated that he had left without having the courtesy to inform me, and instead, decided on his own to send me three junior assistants who looked as clueless as goldfish. I told them how aggravated I was about the way the meeting turned out, and they apologized again, pretending to be sincere about it. Their behaviour was the classic representation of how the top executives in the industry saw innovative techies. Besides, they were the typical ass-licker, yes-men wannabes I have encountered so many times in Hollywood. Anything George Wickham instructed them to do; they would do without question. He could have asked for a lock of my hair and two of them would have held me down while another came at me with sharpened scissors and a menacing grin.

I weighed my options and agreed to do my presentation anyway. When I was finished, they sat in silence with no idea what to say next. The official languages of Belgium are Dutch, German, and French; I might as well have done my presentation in any of them for the response I got. They had no idea what I was talking about. Oh well! After wrapping up all my business meetings for the week, I returned home, turning over in my mind how best to re-strategize my approach with George Wickham. Big Star Agency was so powerful and influential in the industry, that I didn't want to give up easily. George Wickham was a big pion and I wanted to try once more. I decided to email George Wickham and request to schedule a time when we could have a video call. George Wickham agreed and referred me once again to his assistant to make another date. His assistant emailed me and gave me the times when he would be available to speak to me. However, due to the nine - hour time difference between Belgium and Los Angeles, I noticed that all these appointment times were mostly late in the day, close to midnight. But I took one anyway. One meeting was scheduled for 11:00 PM Belgium time, and just five minutes before, I got an email from his assistant telling me:

> *Sorry, George wouldn't be able to attend this meeting. We need to reschedule.*

I could not believe it. I was speechless as I stared at the email with antipathy as if it was some sort of apparition come to life. They knew they were going to cancel, yet they choose to wait until just minutes before the scheduled time before informing me. This was another level of *messed up*. Where was the decency, the respect, and the courtesy that should be the paramount code for business dealings? I was holding up my responsibility, but they didn't care to hold up theirs. However, I rolled with the punches and asked for a new date to be rescheduled. That happened seven times in that cycle and on the seventh time, I stayed up until midnight for the meeting. Only five minutes before the meeting, I got an e-mail from his assistant saying George needed to reschedule once more, and I became so infuriated. I rushed over to my computer and fired off an email:

I get that you are busy and powerful. But your time is no more valuable than mine. If you do not want to talk to me, just say that. Don't waste my time.

This ultra-busy man who never had time to meet with me took the time to respond to that email! He apparently forgot that he told me he was caring for his sick and aging mother. This time, he said he was caring for a sick and aging brother! It seemed he was the only member of his family who wasn't confined to a hospital bed! Lucky guy, I guess! While the rest of his relatives were being struck down in their prime, he was at Starbucks ordering a caramel macchiato! He launched into a lecture on the importance of good manners, boasting about his connections to Hollywood's most powerful figures and warning that he could ruin me with a word. Then he shifted, speaking about keeping life in perspective—handling its ups and downs, and remembering that it's not all about work. He had the nerve to end with a book suggestion about a man who overworked himself to the point of suicide and accused me of being immature and foolish, insisting that someone needed to wake me from the dreamland I was living in. Huh?! This silver-spoon-fed multimillionaire was going to lecture an immigrant who came up from the bottom about hard times? It was time for one more email.

You're going to lecture me about perspective and work? I don't think so! I don't need to put things in perspective because life did that for me. I won't be lectured by a man who grew up in a mansion with his famous family and had his butt wiped by nanny's and maids. I know reality. Reality is my middle name.

With that, the email war was on! He emailed me back and copied multiple executives from various Hollywood companies in an attempt to blacklist me.

> *Nadira, it's a crazy world out there. We need to be more patient with each other. It's not that I don't want to talk to you.*

Suddenly, now that his friends were being cc'd, he took a calm and measured tone. Worse, one of the executives he cc'd was someone we had been working with on a project, jumped into the fray. This person was making a movie with Stephen Spielberg directing. We had analyzed eighteen drafts of their script to determine which one was most viable and didn't charge him a penny. He emailed me and copied the entire group:

> *You are a disgusting human being. This man is my friend. How dare you speak to him in such a manner. I don't want to be connected with you in any way. If you ever so much as say my name, I will sue you!*

All because this horrible dipshit stood me up seven times and I had the audacity to call him on it. I had one more email in me. I cracked my knuckles, rolled my shoulders, and positioned my fingers over the keyboard like an assassin:

> *George Wickham, you're truly a despicable human being for copying others in our conversation. You seem to need a crowd to bully me. You have no*

integrity. There is no other reason for including your powerful friends in a discussion between you and me.

His friend emailed him and copied me on the message. He wrote that George should stop emailing me and should refuse to interact with "garbage." But, to his credit, George Wickham seemed to have some sort of an odd awakening. He replied:

This woman is not garbage. She is smart. She's an entrepreneur. I respect that. This got way out of control.

He directed the next lines of his email to me.

Nadira, I will reschedule and meet you. I promise I will be present. You have my word. Please get in touch.

Shocking. He chastised his friend for getting involved after getting him involved. But by then I was done. I felt like I needed five showers to wash the stench of the interaction off me. I wanted nothing to do with him or any of his friends. The one who jumped in our conversation was bad enough. But even more cowardly were the ones who remained silent. I replied to George's email thus;

That ship has sailed. I don't want to have anything to do with you. I don't want to hear from you. I don't want to interact with you. Not you, or any other person from your friendly little group.

This was my life in dealing with Hollywood, and I was starting to wonder if they were all this way. Were they all so stuck in their ways, so committed to no change, so self-important, so unreliable, that I was wasting my time? And, more importantly, was Hollywood so rotten from the inside that the only salvation for it was death? Perhaps they needed to lose enough money, suffer enough box office flops, that they could no longer afford to put on movies for the world. Perhaps I just needed to wait for the gangrene to make its way from the core to the surface and expose how these people really were. I kept asking myself, "What am I doing trying to work with these people?" I was starting to think that perhaps I was the one who needed to have her head examined.

BORED WITH THE BOARD

By the time 2019 began, there was no question that we had the best product in the world. That fact is undisputed. We considered ourselves done with R & D. The code was able to run itself completely autonomously. We worked with numerous small production companies, yet we still weren't breaking even. My prospect list was overflowing with potential clients, and my inbox was constantly full. On every video call, potential clients recounted their past encounters with our competitors, giving me insight into the challenges they had faced. They called our competitors' AI "voodoo science." Our science was real, and our hard work was paying off.

Our competitors spent more money and effort on their marketing game than their technology. They were hardcore! Their billboards and ads were everywhere. With offices in L.A. and other cities, they were simply more accessible than I was. But the industry started to complain that our competitors' AI models were not good enough. Too many bugs. Too much fake data science. Big error margins. Once film companies tried this one and that one, they were frustrated with artificial results. They came looking to ScriptBook for the real deal. What we lacked in bells and whistles, we made up for in science. The science proved its worth. We were legitimate. But 2019 was a complex year. I hit a low point with my investors. The relationship, that wasn't great to start with, was quickly deteriorating. That deterioration accelerated in 2019. It was like a bad marriage where couples hate the sight of their spouses and sleep with their backs to each other. I think both I and the investors were thinking about separation and perhaps even looking forward to a divorce. I scheduled a board meeting in March and told the board that things were taking off. I explained that we were ready to enter the full-scale marketing and commercialization phase, with the capacity to expand internationally. But the board was already checked out emotionally. It was the strangest meeting. Joe Gazillionaire, the head investor, challenged every word that came out of my mouth. "I know that I am the odd one out in your investment portfolio. You prefer fintech startups and took a leap of faith with me. I serve an industry you know nothing about, and I am the only female CEO in your portfolio. I am building technology that is new in an industry you don't normally invest in. You don't know how to advise me properly." My intent was to put our rocky relationship in context and express my understanding of the many concerns he and the board had.

It was my plan to ask the investors to infuse more money. We were out of runway. We had spent much of the money on R & D. I refused myself any salary beyond what I needed to buy a meal at McDonald's and pay my mortgage. I wasn't going to spend a dollar on myself beyond necessity because I needed every penny to drive the business through its international commercialization phase. I needed more funding. My plan was to use any infusion of additional cash to commercialize and scale. And we desperately needed an office in L.A. with salespeople selling the product locally. I was trying to say that I understood how Joe Gazillionaire felt. But he didn't hear it that way. He heard it as an attack. In short, he went insane! "I don't want to hear your bullshit anymore. You are crazy to think I will put in another dime. Stop lecturing me about my companies. Don't you ever talk to me about my other companies. That's none of your business." The others in the meeting fell silent and looked shocked at the overreaction. At least I knew where I stood. I wasn't going to get another dime. I was on my own. They were pouring good money after bad into the dumbest ventures, but they were not going to support ScriptBook AI even though it had a real shot of success.

I left the meeting wondering what to do next. I had a board in name only. They were not a true board who would advise me, support me, and put money behind the company. They were puppets in the hands of Joe Gazillionaire. By April, I called another board meeting to determine where I stood straight from their lips. "What are your intentions?" I asked like a woman who had been waiting for her boyfriend's marriage proposal for ten years. "The product is ready and needs to be commercialized internationally. You aren't giving me money or advice. Why are you on my board? If you are going to be statues, you are a liability to me." I offered to buy their shares for one dollar each. If they thought my company was worthless, surely, they would sell their stakes. "We will no longer be actively involved in the company," was the response. "We aren't selling our shares because you might hit the jackpot in a year or two. We will be passive board members. You don't have to ask for our permission anymore when you want to do something." Dead weight! I was so thankful I no longer had a board to please — or fail to please. They were out of the picture, so I didn't have to work overtime to gain their approval. They remained uninvolved and unimpressed. At least I would be spared hearing them blathering on and on about orders. Talking to them deflated my spirit; it was tough to preach to the dead. And I ended up with a worse deal than before because I had to carry them! My time with them was marked by their desire to get "more" fast. Quality was to be sacrificed at the altar of immediacy. I couldn't understand how they could be so impatient with their own money. They had so much of it — money, that is — that they seemed perfectly comfortable throwing it around from one investment to the next without ever taking the time to nurture the businesses they invested in or understand the trajectory the businesses should take. The moment they caught a sniff of the minty smell of money, they become ravenous like savages. Their mouths watered and they bared their fangs... at me! They wouldn't have stopped until they got their hands on every dollar they could with no thought to satisfying customers, building trust, and establishing longevity.

I had done my best to reason with them, explaining why it was wise to focus on the AI system and complete that phase before taking orders. It seemed my words were worthless to my investors, which was a dangerous situation for them as well as me. I was the one at the wheel. I was the one setting up and going for meetings, and I knew the executives at the studios more than they could possibly imagine. So, if I decided on a direction for ScriptBook operations, I didn't have to worry that they would overturn it for whatever flimsy reasons they had, digging their own graves. They opted for the long game — waiting it out like they were holding a lottery ticket. If the company did well, they would be the first to benefit, earning at least four times what they put in. But the money problem was not solved. And it *had* to be solved. The ends were not meeting. Before long, payroll would become an issue. Never mind growing the company. I started with deep cost-cutting measures, slicing our expenditures wherever I could. I dipped into my personal savings to infuse ScriptBook with cash. I even turned to my parents for help. Between me and my family members I poured about 150,000 dollars into the company. It was a big ask because my parents were not wealthy by any standard, and the savings I withdrew were all I had.

I regret not paying myself a decent salary. It was a blunder of my novice understanding of the stresses of business. I added my personal stress to the business stress. It was not wise. I would leave the ScriptBook office, weary and worn, only to come home and worry more about whether I would be able to take care of myself. I sold myself short. I worked overtime daily as a matter of course and should have allowed myself to be paid a fair salary. Today, I know better and would advise any startup founder not to put their finances, health, and personal life last. Whether the company succeeds or fails, founders need to maintain their personal financial wellness. On top of the poor decision not to pay myself a regular wage, I went to the bank to secure a loan. I was already in a hole, but I just kept digging it deeper in the attempt to save my company. The bank was optimistic. I left the first meeting with the banker wondering if my board was clinically insane. Here was a bank that is normally cautious about loaning money to startups, showing enthusiasm about approving a loan to me after reviewing our business plan. The loan was big and was approved easily. Between my money, my parent's money, and the bank loan, I had two years of operating capital. I later learned the true weight of those errors on my life long-term.

Up until now, ScriptBook had enjoyed a beautiful office space for its twelve employees. It was located in the center of the city and close to public transit stations. Inside, the office was outfitted with high-end desks and equipment I had purchased with my own money. There were lounge areas where the employees could eat, play cards, and just hang out. I felt this was necessary given the long hours we anticipated spending in that space. At the very least,

I wanted it to be modern and comfortable. My family spent many hours cleaning it, setting it up, decorating, and moving furniture. I remember looking out and seeing my mother, father, sisters rushing about getting the office ready as a labor of love in support of my dreams. My sisters donated their time four times per week cleaning the office. On the weekends, my parents and I went into deep clean. This effort from my family saved my money I would have had to spend on a cleaning service. In that, I was very blessed.

My board never noticed nor cared about the sweat equity we had put in. All the while, the other CEOs in their portfolio were taking lavish trips and scheduling intense team building events courtesy of the money the investors were giving them. When they ran out of money, they placed a call to the investors and got another infusion of cash. No questions asked. I expected the same. However, the reality was that I had no lifeline other than the one I could provide for myself. My next step was to apply for research grants. I did so, but the process of review and approval was so long, it would not help us in the near - term. I could kick myself when I look back at all the mistakes I made. I was a lousy businesswoman supported by a lousy board. So, when the financial tsunami hit our company, we had to surrender that wonderful space in the center of the city and move to a smaller, less expensive space. Telling my team about our financial issues was a difficult conversation. But I had committed myself to always be transparent with the team, refusing to keep them in the dark. They were more than employees. They were friends. We spent the majority of our lives together over those years. I owed them the truth. "The board has cut us off," I said pensively. "We have enough money to get us through the next two years. But we will have to move."

I contacted an entrepreneur who had a company that was larger than mine. He was running a tech company that crossed the globe from Belgium, throughout Europe and into Singapore and China. He housed 200 employees in a massive space. His company was growing well, in part, because of investments by the same firm I relied on to help me: Joe Gazillionaire! I approached this man about subleasing some of his office space to me. I told him that the investors had dropped me and I was fighting for survival. He responded favorably and invited us to come. When I asked what he might charge, I was shocked at the price. It was a fraction of what I expected. The price was so low, I initially thought he was joking. Furthermore, the rent included all the utilities like electricity and water. The true caliber of friendship is measured on our worst days. This man came to my rescue like a knight in shining armor, and I will never forget his generosity. We had not been lifelong friends, having only met a few times at Gazillionaire's networking events where he gathered his CEOs together. But he understood my struggle and wanted to be a part of my success story. Furthermore, the space he gave us was pristine. It was large enough for my team to have the space they needed, with a large room for our servers, and conference rooms we could use as needed. He was a gentleman, and I am forever grateful to him.

I expected we would stay only a couple of months, because I did not want to impede his ability to grow and expand his operation into the space we were using. But he never pressured us to leave and allowed us to extend our stay as long as we needed. Beyond the material blessings he offered, he was also a support for me as an entrepreneur. He freely shared his best practices and offered advice whenever I needed it. He identified with the struggles I was having with Joe Gazillionaire and shared my disdain for the man, relaying the details of a massive fight the two had when they disagreed over the direction of the company. The meeting ended when this man told Gazillionaire to "shove it." He refused to be threatened and told Gazillionaire he could have his investment back. He wrote Gazillionaire a check for 10 million dollars and told him to "get the hell out of his company." He had been wise enough to diversify his funding so, when Gazillionaire became difficult with him, he had other places to turn. This man was a master salesman and had a talent for getting rich people to write big checks.

By the summer of 2019, I had a lot to be thankful for and a lot to worry about. The team was working harder than ever and doing a masterful job and our new office was a treasure along with the added benefit of a new friend and mentor as a landlord. On the other hand, I had a passive board that was no longer willing to invest money, resources, or guidance for my business. Ah, the board. To say that my board let me down is the understatement of the century. When I was working so hard, putting in long hours, one might suspect that one person might have checked in to see how I was faring under intense scrutiny and extraordinary pressure. The behavior of the board was quite puzzling since, besides me, they had the most to lose. After all, it was their money on the line. You would think that they would invest some time into making sure their "key man," or in this case, their "key woman" was faring well. But there wasn't a single call… not a visit or a lunch. Nothing! They seemed to forget (or didn't care) that I was a human being, a new entrepreneur, and a trailblazer. Having walked this road before, they certainly should have known the size of the weight I was carrying. Still, there wasn't any interest in my humanity. I had depleted my savings and owed the bank and my parents a princely sum.

Big clients and substantial sales started coming our way, while many proof - of - concept projects with the major studios were still underway. By September, we were working with four major film studios: Mercury Studios, Saturn Pictures, Venus Studios, and

Jupiter Pictures. Film production companies were finding us and asking to do paid trials. But none of the four studios wanted to pay during the proof – of – concept phase. I take full responsibility for that. I should have insisted that they have skin in the game. A functional and supportive board might have helped me take such a stand. Because the studios were receiving something of value over the space of twelve to eighteen months of work, I should have at least insisted that they cover my operational costs. In addition to our regular operating costs and server costs, we required legal representation to negotiate the agreements with each studio and had to purchase many expensive insurance policies to satisfy the studios.

Nothing comes for free. It is a lesson I later learned. By letting them go through the proof – of – concept for free, I devalued the extreme benefit they were receiving. The studios repeatedly assured us that they intended to sign commercial agreements with ScriptBook AI. With letters of intent in hand, I fully expected that these trials would culminate in multi-million dollar contracts. If we were successful with the studio's trials, I reasoned, we would be making millions in a year in revenue. We were surviving on the loan I had taken out, my savings, and a loan from my parents. In addition, I was waiting on a research grant. Spending so much on proof – of – concept projects came at a high cost, but we did it with the hope of reaping substantial rewards down the line.

2020 was sailing... at least at the beginning. We were doing well with our ongoing proof – of – concepts and relatively impressive sales with other production companies and film funds. The invitations continued to pour in for ScriptBook AI to feature at tech and film events. There was a shift happening in the film industry. Companies were starting to wake up to the strengths of

AI. And my hopes were riding high. I might just fix my broken finances on my own, without the help of my investors. I felt as if I had less stress with the board out of the picture. I no longer had to feel the heat of their breath on my neck. It was freeing.

One day I got a shocking call from a huge private equity firm, BBB Capital. They had billions in assets and were notorious for writing nine-figure investment checks. They heard about ScriptBook AI and were convinced that the entertainment world would move toward AI driven decision support systems and wanted to get their hat in the ring as an investor. To sweeten the pot, they are majority stakeholders in many Hollywood film studios and talent agencies. So they had a lot of gain from ScriptBook's success. I chatted with some of their London partners. The conversation went well and led to additional conversations. Then, they dropped the bomb that they were not interested in investing necessarily. One of the partners had a group of Oscar winning screenwriters and directors he met with regularly. At one of their meetings, they had come up with some ideas about how ScriptBook AI could support that group of high-profile players in the industry. He invited me to London. Of course, I was thrilled to come. I was only a two-hour train ride from London, and I was interested in the concept. But I wanted to meet on a day when I could stack several other meetings in London as well.

I contacted Pie Group, one of the biggest media groups in the UK, and arranged a time to see them. We had analyzed hundreds of historical movies for them and a dozen of their new film projects. We planned to review the results our AI system returned to Pie Group. With four meetings in place, I planned a daytrip. I arranged for a flight to London to minimize the travel time. My flight was scheduled to leave at 6:30 Wednesday morning. By Monday, I was feeling ill. By Tuesday, I could hardly get out of bed. My condition worsened by the hour. I had not been that sick in years. I felt like I was drifting in and out of consciousness. It was time to alert the team. I asked one of my colleagues to fly out and take the meeting with BBB Capital. It was a once – in – a – lifetime opportunity. The rest of my team was competent, and we discussed everything. I never needed to bring anyone up to speed. They could step in my place at a moment's notice. By the end of the day Tuesday, I was in the emergency room. On Wednesday my colleague conducted the meetings in London, but they didn't go well. At BBB Capital, the partner was disappointed that I wasn't there despite being told that I was in the hospital. He emotionally checked out and he behaved rudely to my colleague. The Pie Group meeting was a failure as well. My colleague described the meeting as a "conference room full of dummies." The people present had no background in tech, leaving him stunned at their level of ignorance.

Plans were already in place for me to fly to L.A. next week, where I would meet with a couple of film studios and several production companies. Two of the four studios we were working with were ready to discuss the results of our proof - of - concept trials. I suggested completing the meeting as a video call. But one of the executives of Mercury Studios explained that the CEO was not a fan of such conversation over video. So, barely on my feet again, I packed for Los Angeles. I did everything I could to nurse myself back to health so that I would be coherent for the trip. But as the days passed, I was pale, dehydrated, shivering, and unsteady on my feet. I poured medications and vitamins down my throat. By next Monday, I was on a plane to L.A. with a colleague. I slept the entire twelve hours. We laid over in Dublin and tried to grab a bite. But I couldn't even get a salad down. By the time we reached the hotel I was exhausted. I could hardly speak, struggled to breathe, and couldn't do any prep for the meetings.

I went to the Mercury Studios meeting and did my best to pretend to be okay. My colleague was overjoyed to be there. She had never been to the film studios and was wide-eyed at it all. After she took a few pictures, we headed to the offices. At the meeting, we discussed the proof - of - concept accuracy rates, and their request that the reports would be exportable to Excel. Excel was the bane of my existence. It was a horrible program to work with and I could never understand why people would take such sophisticated data and slap it onto an Excel spreadsheet. Excel, to me, is like a virus we will never rid ourselves of. The meeting was scheduled with the CEO of Mercury Studios. We had already done a proof – of - concept two years earlier on a smaller scale, but many of the leadership in Mercury Studios was new, which made the work we had done in the past invalid. The one executive who remained told us we would have to start from scratch.

We waited in the conference room until the door swung open and they all filed in. Suddenly the Big Cheese came in. I watched as the mood in the room changed. People worshipped him. It was very old-fashioned. I wasn't impressed. To me, he was just another man in his jeans, a sweater, and a cap on his head. He was dressed decades away from his age. He started a conversation about his weekend that lasted far too long. I could feel the heat rising in me. I had dragged my sick body across the ocean, on a flight for twelve hours just to meet him. And he was talking about the pimple on his forehead that he had to cover with his cap. I wanted to vomit all over his ugly clothes! I explained the proof – of – concept and started the debrief. I compared and contrasted their internal accuracy rates against ScriptBook's accuracy. ScriptBook was kicking their ass. But I wasn't surprised. The reputation at Mercury Studios was poor, even internally.

The CEO was so immature and unfocused, it was like making a presentation to a toddler. He fired questions at me so fast but then didn't even wait to listen to the answer. As soon as I opened my mouth to speak, he was already teed up with new questions. He was like a puppy bouncing around me. It made me more nauseous than the fever I was battling. He mentioned that Mercury Studios passed on the movie "Knives Out" and asked what ScriptBook AI predicted. I explained that ScriptBook predicted the movie would be a huge success (which it was). Had they had ScriptBook AI, they would have never passed. He then informed about the movie "The Rhythm Section", which they had also chosen to pass on. The same was true for Blake Lively's "The Rhythm Section" which ScriptBook AI predicted would flop. It did.

There was nothing to criticize about the product except that the AI was better at doing his job of hitting winners than he was. Mercury Studio 's greenlight success rate was twenty-eight percent and ScriptBook's success rate was over eighty percent. The movie studio executives exposed themselves as highly immature because they were unable to accept a reality that was being proven to them. Acceptance is the key and one of the hardest things for people to achieve. It takes maturity to accept that something or someone is better than you and then allow them to do it. In this case, Mercury Studios saw ScriptBook AI as a rival. I instinctively knew right there and then that Mercury Studios would never sign with us. There it was — the result of the debrief. Twelve months of hard work, done for free, and I was watching it slip straight down the drain.

My calendar was packed with meetings, but at the forefront of my mind was film studio number two: Venus Pictures. The next day we left the hotel early to have breakfast. I couldn't even swallow my coffee. I watched jealously as my colleague downed her avocado toast. Looking back, I wonder if I had not contracted COVID long before it was prevalent. I was travelling so much, I might have easily caught the virus. At the Venus Pictures meeting, I struggled to get words out of my mouth. There were six people at the meeting, and each was knowledgeable about tech. They were more professional than Mercury Studios and understood data analytics. The feedback from Venus Pictures was positive. They were very happy with the results of the proof - of - concept. They asked us to run multiple drafts of fifty new film projects. They asked about casting and how it might change the results. This was more like it. We walked out of the meeting with pictures of Venus on the screen behind us and word that legal would reach out to start drafting the commercial contract. Relief washed over me. I was happy, but the fever dulled everything, leaving me unable to show it.

One thing I could never quite understand about some of the other studios was how the heads of Technology, Innovation, Data Science, and similar departments had landed their positions. Virtually no one had a degree in a technology related field. These people were History majors, English majors, Political science majors. No engineers. No data science background. How were these people running the technology departments at movie studios? It was an insult to anyone like me who developed AI. Having a conversation with someone with an English background is like a professional chef explaining to me, a non-cook, how to cream butter. These folks were in their positions for years. Their knowledge was not hands-on; they made decisions based entirely on hearsay.

DUE DILIGENCE

I was desperate to ensure that ScriptBook AI was not a flash in the pan or a one hit wonder. I had seen so many companies come out of the gate fast, but they weren't strong enough to go the distance. They rounded the bend, ran out of steam, and fell behind the pack. There was something those companies didn't know or didn't have. Some of the CEOs of those failing companies understood why they failed. Others were still scratching their heads. That knowledge kept me sharp and alert. Before we undertook any new projects, the film studios pressured us into being vetted extensively, taking us through a rough due diligence process complete with audits. Such was the case when a tech company – turned – movie studio reached out, intrigued by what our product could offer. This movie studio, Metaverse Studios, was doing their due diligence as well. They demanded a background check on each one of our employees. That part of the due diligence process took nearly four months — a whole four months to be vetted and approved by several divisions. They had done background checks on our employees who were not even working in the United States. At times, I wondered if we were in the business of helping to get movies made, or if we were going to be working directly for the President of the United States and would be stationed right in the White House. The whole process involved a series of insurances we had to purchase to protect the interest of other companies. Complying with that requirement cost us a great deal of money as a company. At the time, we were barely breaking even. So, writing checks for thousands upon thousands of dollars for contracts and insurances was tough. But it was required before they would even release the scripts to us to analyze. The board was right about one thing: it would have been nice to make much more money. We were laying out large sums on a regular basis and seeing little in return. I was ready to go the distance. But I could feel the hot breath of the Board on my neck wondering when the money was going to flow in rather than out.

Looking back, the investors could not have been more passive in ensuring their investment generated a return. If, for example, they had made the decision to channel in more funds — like they were doing with the other companies that weren't half as far along as ScriptBook — we would have been able to properly commercialize our activities in the highly competitive market. The game changer would have been to establish a base in Los Angeles and start a huge sales and marketing campaign there. Hollywood only respects its own. If you are not in the U.S., you have one big strike against you. If you are not in L.A., that's strike two. One more strike and… well, you know. It was only a matter of perspective. If the board could have wrapped their minds around the potential, despite the risk, they might have seized the possibility of the profit it could yield. We might then have been able to close seven-figure deals. Had they been guiding me properly, they might have encouraged me to start selling right away on a smaller scale. If we had the right financial backing, I wouldn't have needed to wait until the AI was completed. We had smaller fish to fry that kept us going while we sat in our boat trying to reel in "the big one." I wish they had put ScriptBook in a position to hire a team of salespeople in the U. S.

to sell what we had. It would have been gobbled up like hot cakes. Then I would have been getting orders while I was perfecting the system. By the time the major motion picture studios got around to completing their Proof - of - Concept and all the other hoops we had to jump through, they would have been receiving thousands of scripts that were ScriptBook certified! It would have pushed them to make the big purchase we were all hoping for. But, without funds to move my life, my business, and my staff to L.A., I opted to stay in Belgium and finish the AI before starting to sell. The lack of big sales caused the board to see us as a failing prospect.

As soon as I returned from my trip to L.A., it was time for the Berlin International Film Festival. At the same time, there were rising concerns about COVID. I had several meetings booked at the Berlin Film Market. We offered closed demos of the product to several film finance funds. Practically every company ordered; some placed small orders with promises of large orders later. I was hopeful again. ScriptBook AI was really taking off. Acquisitions and mergers were being discussed. We had lots of options and optimism was the order of the day. We had done very little marketing, yet companies were finding us quite easily. But I wanted to accelerate. Growing organically is nice for flowers. I wanted to grow like a weed on speed. Technology was about timing, and we couldn't afford to arrive too late for the party. I needed to employ salespeople in the U. S. and gear up my marketing game. I had even begun scouting office space in L.A. My team and I bandied about ideas as we tried to decide our best next step.

BBB Capital contacted me again. The representative said that a group of investors wanted to put money in technology and were looking at ScriptBook AI. This high-profile group envisioned technology that would allow a next-generation writers' room to become a place where talent would be cultivated in a way with the help of AI, and they were looking at ScriptBook to do this. Steve Knight of *Peaky Blinders* was said to be one of the interested parties along with some Oscar winning screenwriters and directors. I was prepared to talk about that. Just as I was about to leave, Belgium was locked down due to COVID. If I traveled to London, I might be stuck there and not permitted to return. It was a risk. A day later, just about all of Europe had instituted travel bans. My plans were cancelled. I contacted Steve Knight and the gang and told them I could not travel to London to do the meeting. This was the second time the meeting with BBB Capital & Co was being cancelled. The first time we had planned to meet, I had been sick. Now there was a lockdown. I suggested a conference call. One of the partners at BBB Capital insisted that the meeting happen in Soho House in London so we could spend several hours together, have lunch, talk about technology, plan, share vision, brainstorm, etc. I understood. This wasn't something for the phone. But these were extraordinary conditions. Suddenly the air was escaping from my balloon, and I felt like I was sinking. But we did have the meeting via conference call and Steve Knight was extremely interested and lovely to talk to. He shared his vision for a next-generation writers' group and wanted to be involved from conception to fruition. He thought he would cultivate the next generation of successful writers. Noble! Not many people think about others. I was impressed. We talked for an hour before we got weary of the call. We ended our time together by promising to think about next steps. But we never got together again. It was a missed opportunity. Thanks, COVID!

After that, the entertainment world shut down. Movie theatres closed. Studio lots were shuttered. Film festivals and markets were postponed. We went into a dark winter where the only entertainment available was on streaming platforms. In April and May, I started receiving emails from writers and filmmakers asking if ScriptBook AI still offered the four - page PDF report from years ago. The answer was yes. We still offered the four - page script analysis for $199. With the lockdown, everyone had time on their hands and wanted to perfect their scripts. The emails struck a nerve. I had offered the exact same product through the Black List partnership for half the price. Now writers were asking for my help.

Many of the people who contacted me admitted they had no money. They were already struggling, but with restaurants and other places of business closed down or scaled down, many of them were out of a job. It tugged at my heartstrings, and I talked to my team about ways we could help for less money or even for free. With that, the COVID script marketplace was born. Yes, I could have thought of a better name. We sometimes called it the Solidarity Market. I made it open and free for people to enter their information and upload their scripts, and they would get a large chunk of the analysis for free. We posted on social media and created newsletters. Thousands of projects were uploaded to the Covid script marketplace. Everything was encrypted to protect the writers' copyright. I even added something extra. Scripts that ranked high in the scores, I marked as high potential and passed them on to my contacts in the industry. There was no charge and no kickback to us. It was just a charitable effort from ScriptBook AI to the writers and filmmakers community. The producers and executives I sent the scripts to were actually reading them when they learned it received a high ScriptBook score. So much for shady Belgians. I wanted to increase this charitable venue. I reached out to the sites known for screenwriting competitions, script evaluation, guilds and organizations, and many other sites from coast to coast. I invited them to send their clients our way for a free analysis. But they were too afraid to collaborate with us. Even during COVID, none of them were interested in sharing in this charitable drive. Hollywood had no heart… no soul.

Even after I had been burned by the screenwriters, I wanted to help them. But I was alone. I kept it free until the end of 2020, offering nearly a year's worth of service and analyzing thousands of scripts. ScriptBook AI had a vault of film projects that were curated and validated by our AI. I guess about ten to fifteen percent of the uploaded film projects were marked as high commercial potential by our AI. This meant that our covid script marketplace had quite a few potential blockbusters waiting to be picked up. I prayed for a first look deal with a production company or a studio but I had no idea how to go about getting this type of venture off the ground so I kept giving. I was checking out the competition on the internet to see if ScriptBook AI was getting any negative feedback. Large numbers of people were praising ScriptBook AI. For the ones who continued to spew poison online, I emailed them and let them know they were banned on Scriptbook. They would never be allowed to use ScriptBook AI again. Rather than retreat to their swamp in shame, they went back on social media and complained about being banned.

A HAIL MARY

One of the last movies we predicted was for a big project starring an all-star cast. We analyzed twelve different drafts of the script. That really highlighted the power of ScriptBook AI. When it was fully built out, it was able to quantify potential box office based on storyline variation. The script was (ironically enough) written by Craig Mazin (from *Chernobyl*) who torched ScriptBook AI during our partnership with The Black List. After running our analysis on all twelve drafts of the script, the predicted box office was below expectations on each variation. The nine executives present for the pitching of the results looked worried. So, they asked us to play around with additional suggested cast members to see which star actors would increase box office predictions. In one draft of the script, they wanted us to match star actor X with star actress Y. In another, they wanted to try star actor Z. None of this worked because our research showed over and over again that star power has little effect on box office predictions. It is the strength of the story — the power of the script — that impacts financial projections. We explained this to the nine execs, doing our best to educate them that the quality of the storytelling is the only thing that significantly impacts how high the financials tick. No star actor would create a jump in the box office predictions. They could take the two biggest actors in Hollywood, pair them with a bad script, and the movie will flop. In fact, the reverse of their theory was likely true: the bigger the star power, the higher the moviegoer's expectations. Placing a big name as the headliner only demanded an even bigger blockbuster. The executives flew into a visible rage. They were furious with ScriptBook — my team and me — for giving this honest answer. After the meeting ended, the execs began to quote the line of the truly desperate: "We'll always have the China box office. China will fix the disappointing US box office projections." This is how Hollywood works. But it wasn't my job to make the decision for them. My role was to give them the data they needed to use to make their decision. I was just happy to have been given the meeting.

Before I knew it, we were ringing in the New Year. It was 2021 and COVID was nowhere near over huffing and puffing and blowing our houses down. We had completed the extensive proof – of – concept projects for the remaining two major film studios. We were working with film funds that we signed with at the Berlin Film Market and had ongoing projects with small scale production companies. After completing the proof - of - concepts with the final studios, it became clear that no one was going to sign a commercial deal, at least not until the cinemas were open for business again. Hollywood was closed and studios were releasing their new titles on streaming platforms. Many had put projects on hold until the pandemic was over. ScriptBook AI was a low priority. This was bad news because we had invested so much money and time for the last 18 months. Bad timing? Bad luck? The perfect storm? Yes, all of the above.

I started to become very worried. It was the first time the alarm bells sounded so loudly, my ears were ringing constantly. After all, we still weren't making a profit, and I had kept the company afloat for almost two years on the money from the infusion of cash from my savings, the loan from the bank and our modest sales. We needed big contracts. We needed the seven - figure deals that only big studios could provide. The sales we did score helped us break even. But that wasn't enough. We had taken out loans that needed to be repaid. Only a seven-figure deal would save the day.

The European Union agreed to release billions of dollars to support companies that were struggling during COVID. These were convertible loans. Belgium received a slice of that money. Every tech company jumped on it because they needed cash. I prepared the required proposal as well as the notarized documentation that had to accompany the application. I spent upwards of $10,000 just to get the paperwork done to apply for the COVID loan. I requested one million dollars. Other tech companies reported a high success rate. The loans were being administered through the same public VC fund that had invested in me: Dray M. It was EU-owned, funded by taxes. The people who worked there called themselves venture capitalists. But they were bureaucrats. They did not know the first thing about running a company and what our needs were. Still, I was hopeful. A million dollars would get us through another seven months and possibly through the end of COVID. The waiting period was three months due to a backlog of applications. In the meantime, Hollywood started firing employees. And many who weren't fired decided to quit. Working from home was in vogue and people discovered they could use technology to make money in their pajamas.

Streaming platforms were popping up like popcorn. Companies that had previously turned their noses up at the idea of streaming were now launching. They were the big winners of the COVID crisis. Many high-ranking executives saw the trend and left the studios to join tech companies. My email inbox was filled with auto-responses that people I was trying to reach at the studios no longer worked there. A quick Google search uncovered that they had gone to work for tech entertainment companies. These same execs who hated our AI, decided to jump ship and become execs at film tech startups — essentially working for our competition. All of a sudden, the execs sitting across the table had changed sides. It was the height of hypocrisy for those execs to be selling AI software to the same studios they had worked at before when they were fighting off AI like they were at war with a band of marauding Vikings!

Our U.S. based competitors were issuing press release after press release about the employees they had managed to snag from Hollywood during the COVID crisis. It was like bizarro world. Hollywood execs who had shunned tech were now helping to move tech forward. It was a big win for our US-based competition because they were able to get these executives at a discount. Part of me wanted to be in America where all the action was. But the lockdown meant I couldn't leave Belgium. In my native language, Dutch, we call it Black Snow. It's what happens when you hit storm after storm, but instead of fluffy white snow, it's piles of shit falling from the sky. Suddenly, the people I once had to pitch to were on my side. My competitors were closing seven figure deals! The software wasn't even close to ScriptBook's AI. But I wasn't in America. I didn't have the money to hire representatives in the states to work for me. Deals were flying around like paper in a ticker tape parade. And I was left to watch it from afar with a sour feeling in the pit of my stomach. I explained this situation to Dray M, who was managing the Covid funding, hoping they would understand that I needed the funds to stay in the game. I begged them to expedite my application. But they snored back at me. I shook them, but I couldn't wake them from their slumber. A few weeks later, I marched into Dray M's offices to demand an answer. Yes or no?! I had met all the requirements to ensure that my fiscal and legal documents were in place. I discovered that my proposal had never actually been submitted— it had been left to decay, either sitting unnoticed in someone's inbox or gathering dust on a desk. No decision-maker had seen it. If looks could kill, I would be a felon. The representative consoled me by saying that I would never have been given the loan anyway. Mine was not the kind of company they were anxious to save.

The summer of 2021 was a depressing time. The blossoms blooming around me were like death wreaths, and the birds singing their morning songs were like a funeral dirge. For the first time, I realized that bankruptcy was on the horizon. If something big didn't happen fast, it would be over. My business vision was already adapted to the changing climate in Hollywood. I was well-placed to meet the need. But I was absent and helpless. However, I wasn't beaten. I envisioned a biosphere that would remove the fragmentation happening in the industry and democratize a space where buyers and sellers of film projects came together. Our technology would be able to curate and validate every script and every project.

By the end of the summer of 2021, I was still not speaking to my board. Dray M advised that I had limited funds (No shit, Sherlock). They told me I had to either find a new investment or file for bankruptcy. They refused to invest anything more in my company. "Give us a call when you are ready to file for bankruptcy." How mentally constipated does one have to be to give this sort of advice. But that was my support system. I started to search for someone who might want to merge with ScriptBook AI or purchase the company. I was more interested in selling than merging. At the same time, I searched for new investors. Usually, when you decide to sell your company, the board prepares a prospectus and hires an investment bank. But I had Dray M— the nothing group. I took meeting after meeting until my stress level was so high, it made me long for the drama of co-founders.

I was in a dark September. My emotions were all over the place. Gone was the young, bright-eyed woman with hope and promise radiating from her lovely face. She had been replaced by an aged and weathered version of herself, beaten down by exhaustion, doubt, betrayal, and the cares of life. Life had carved deep wrinkles in her brow and inverted her natural smile. Her eyes were bloodshot. She was terrifying. She was terrified. I was broken in some ways. I was stronger in other ways. I lost as much as I gained. I was weaker in the areas that mattered… but hardened. All of the things that keep us young — hope, wonder, excitement, adventure — were crushed and replaced with suspicion, mistrust, and reality.

My family took a stand and said it was too painful for them to ride the rollercoaster with me. So, I stopped updating them. My only outlet was gone. I had to hold it all inside. I received acquisition offers. So, my problems should have been over. I would get a large sum of money and be hired for a role within. But I couldn't pull the trigger on any one of them. They had other plans for ScriptBook AI, and I couldn't agree to sell it knowing what they were planning to do with it. Millions of lines of code would be cut in pieces and destroyed. My original intent would be lost. The investors would be paid back, but there was hardly anything left for me. Even though I invested my own money in the company, I was the last to be paid. The exit clause in the original term sheet made the outcome painfully clear: the investors would walk away with four times their money, and I would be left destitute. My answer was no. I turned to the merger offers, realizing it would take many more months to complete. But I was facing money shortages. I was facing not making payroll!

Another group of investors appeared and offered something interesting. Combined, the investors wanted to do a series A - round of five million dollars to start. The investors were famous Belgian politicians who courted me for weeks. They saw what my investors didn't see. I was impressed with their vision and understanding of the intersection of tech and entertainment. I told them the whole sordid story, and they knew I was close to bankruptcy. I heard the angels sing. I had my miracle. But things are never what they seem. By the third meeting, I learned their true mission. One of them wanted to take over as CEO. Fair enough. But they wanted me to work as the CEO, the CTO, and Head of Data Science while they paraded around getting the press and glory. Just like politicians do. They wanted to saddle me with three different roles while they didn't come to work at all. It was a crap deal… but I seriously considered it. I made a counteroffer. I wasn't the naïve little woman who had started this venture. I was not born yesterday. The term sheet was an insult, and I knew it. I took it home, pondered it carefully, and returned with something that was more respectful of the work I had done and would have to do. The counteroffer was more beneficial to everyone involved. But they didn't agree.

I sat in my car as the sounds and sights of Christmas filled the air. I was too exhausted for tidings of comfort and joy. Nothing comforted me. Joy was a foreign word. All I knew was exhaustion — exhaustion from racing time. For the past nine months, I had sped down the track hoping to save my company before time crossed the finish line of bankruptcy. But time was edging ahead, so I ran harder. Two days after Christmas, I told my family I didn't see any way forward. I would have to close the company. I had a similar conversation with my employees who I had been updating all along since the summer. Everyone encouraged me. They knew the hell I had been through.   Once I said it out loud, I thought the weight would lift. But it just became heavier. So heavy, in fact, I ended up in bed for a few days barely willing to lift my head. It had been a long, tough run. And I had been beaten. I would not greet the New Year with party hats, noisemakers, and resolutions. I would greet it with lawyers. ScriptBook AI would be no more.

PARTY LIKE IT'S 1999

On January 1, 2022, ScriptBook AI filed for bankruptcy. It was a hell of a way to start what was supposed to be a pinnacle year in my life. But there was no denying the sinking of the ship beneath the crashing waves. The company had been taking on water at an alarming rate. I was soaked from head to toe. The end of ScriptBook AI became official and the new reality for me. Even though the warnings about this reality had been visible for a while, it did little to prepare me for the impact, particularly because everyone else was ushering in the new year with laughter and happiness, with hope and anticipation. I was tempted to snatch the party hats off their silly little heads and ram them down their celebratory throats. I was suffering and wanted everyone's sympathy. Though no one's sympathy would serve as the salve I needed to soothe my pain.

The celebration of the New Year was way different for me. I was like the Civil War soldiers who got shot on their way home after the war was over. Tragic. Ironic. Sad. Imagine the whole world celebrating the end of the war as you lay on a medic's gurney dying a slow death. Yep, that was me. And for it all to happen at the beginning of 2022 was especially achy. While everyone was reveling in the festivities of the New Year, emerging from punishing lockdowns, happy to have survived COVID, making and granting wishes, exchanging full frontal kisses, crafting grand and small plans, making unrealistic resolutions they wouldn't keep until February, I was going through a delicate and sensitive moment in my life. I had just lost ScriptBook forever. I was going through the extraordinary waves of grief in the best way I could after having buried the baby I birthed, nurtured, loved, and tried to save. This was death. So, the activities of the people around me were puzzling even though they were completely normal.

> *How can they just go on? It's not fair! How can they laugh and smile and drink like the world isn't coming to an end? Can't they see this is a wake? Why aren't they dressed in black and singing mourning songs? These folks are singing Prince declaring that they are going to "party like it's 1999!"*

I've had ample time to think and reflect on my life, especially the last seven years. Since the loss of my company — my dream — I often find myself trying to figure out what went wrong. Where, exactly, did everything begin to go downhill for the company? Psychotic, I know, but I felt as if I had to pinpoint the exact moment when the rocket speeding straight up lost momentum and fire, hung in midair for a millisecond, and then started its descent into the ocean. I won't say I got a divine revelation to the many questions that rolled around in my mind like loose marbles during those dark, sad days. Nor will I claim there was an exact answer to any of the questions. There were just flashes of moments. Moments that might have been the beginning of the end. Things I should have said. Things I shouldn't have done. Places where I took a stand that perhaps called for a compromise and vice versa. But none of those moments seemed to answer the "why" question. After all, this was the idea of a lifetime. This was as big as Facebook, as big as Tesla, as big as Amazon! Ok, maybe not. But it was at least as big as that company with the robot vacuum cleaner that runs around picking up your cracker crumbs. That company was pulling in hundreds of millions. Mine was bankrupt. As I said, the demise of ScriptBook AI didn't catch me by surprise. Still, I decided I had to land on a decision about its cause of death. If I didn't, sleep would continue to elude me, and my future prospects would slip through my fingers like sand. Here is what I decided.

I believe ScriptBook AI ended the way it did because of a combination of factors that accumulated over the final twelve months. I arrived at this conclusion all on my own, although I briefly considered seeking the skilled divination of a spiritualist or, at least, the super analysis of an AI to work out what went wrong and why. Like a detective, I needed to walk myself down the paths surrounding this heinous and senseless murder until I got to the spot where the truth fell at my feet. Unlike in criminal cases, though, the truth of the death of a company is far more subjective. Business analysts reviewing my case might come to different conclusions. I came to my own. My truth.

Looking past all the ways in which I was naïve, foolish, or inexperienced, I have had to ponder all of the other facets of my business that did not go according to plan. My investors. My co-founders. My board. The screenwriters. The movie industry. The list was broad and long. I don't have the words to describe how disappointed I was in the people who were charged with helping me make decisions and grow the company. The many combined factors leading to ScriptBook's bankruptcy were only recognizable in its entirety when I got completely detached from the company. Like looking at an intricate painting, I needed to take a giant step back so I could see the totality of it. Only when I wasn't submerged in the whole process any longer, could I lend a critical eye to what went wrong. In order to do that, though, I nearly had to separate my mind from my spirit.

Thinking about my business — my baby — always conjured up a stew of emotions from mourning to anger. I had to divorce myself from it all to offer a fair opinion. No biases, no guises and, of course, no false hopes. I was free to see things differently from who I was as the CEO and founder of ScriptBook AI. And this, for me, is far more important, especially in a difficult moment of mourning. So, I went through the motions of grief the best way I could. There are stages of grief… My heart heavy in my chest and fighting to hold back a torrent of tears, I trudged through those stages like a bull in line waiting to be castrated. These were dark moments in my life, and I wish I could say I was resolutely strong in the face of grief. I wish I could say grieving was easy to deal with, especially when it doesn't involve a human being I was close to and loved dearly. I wish I could tell you the affirmations I used to get me through it with grace and charm. You're OK. I'm OK. Scratch that. I am definitely *not* OK.

None of the business books tell you how to navigate bankruptcy while maintaining your sanity and self-esteem. There is no *Bankruptcy for Dummies*. There are just dummies who wander the streets wondering what they are supposed to do with their days after their company goes bust. What to do… What to think… What to feel… Grieving the loss of my brother taught me some things, but it didn't make me immune to grief. Not at all. It still hurt. I was still forced to wrestle with the pain. However, the process of grieving hit me differently than what I expected. It's not like the problems ScriptBook faced eluded me. The fate of the company was visible to me and the investors for quite a while, and the grieving process definitely had an antecedent. But when it eventually arrived in its full force, it wasn't any easier to bear. Even though I tried to build some shock absorbers around me, they crumbled into nothing in the face of the real thing.

I had run ScriptBook AI for seven long, roller coaster years. I had worked so hard without any form of respite or recompense. I believed. I hoped. I dreamed. I even fantasized. It's only natural that I mourned when the whole enterprise came to nothing. ScriptBook AI. It was my brainchild and I nurtured it as a mother would her baby. Even with its many disabilities, I still cared deeply about ScriptBook and the hopes and dreams it held. ScriptBook was far more than a money-making proposition. I believed it would improve — dare I say, revolutionize — the entertainment industry, democratize the Hollywood scene, and better the consumer's experience. There was no loser in this proposition. But I forgot about the mammoth-sized egos in Hollywood. Therein, lay my first mistake. All the other mistakes were just derivatives of that first giant error. Now I was buried in paperwork up to my eyeballs to lay ScriptBook to rest. Going bankrupt in Belgium is nothing like going bankrupt in the United States. In the States, the concept of failing in business is not stigmatized. In fact, entrepreneurs are praised for their valiant effort and give speeches about what they learned. You get up and try again. The culture in Belgium, and in many other European cultures, treats bankruptcy like a crime and failed business owners like criminals. Bankruptcy is done in hiding and the mourning is done in silence.

I was glad the nightmare was over. I had started ScriptBook with passion, hope, and ambition. I was bringing democratization to Hollywood. But I was also bringing equality and justice. I stood up to Goliath. And he crushed me like a bug. I would not get to David in the story. Not this time. On the back end, I felt the hangover of my ambition. I spent the whole of January in my apartment afraid to come outside… afraid everyone would see the scarlet letter B for bankrupt on my forehead. I just wrapped my robe tighter and tighter around my body each day, afraid to put on clothes. Putting on clothes for what? To go outside? To talk to other human beings about the weather? Getting dressed meant engaging with the world. I wasn't about to do that. It was clear I needed therapy. So, I decided to write this book as my first act of healing myself.

Putting this story on paper allowed me to let go. I had been feeling physical pain in my chest and shoulders. I had cried before these final days and months, but I hadn't released those raw, pent up, bitter tears. Even the loss of my brother was mixed in with all the emotions somehow. It was all inside. It all had to come out. I was disappointed in life. I was disappointed in humanity. The ideals of justice and equality were as dead to me as ScriptBook. The world needed to know what I had experienced. Suffering in silence is noble. But it's not me. There were days I could only cry, days I could only laugh, and days when the tears were happy tears. I wondered what I might do with the rest of my life. I confess, I swore off ambition forever. I promised to never put myself through this hell again. But entrepreneurs are magnetically drawn to the prospect of commercial success and empire-building. We are blessed (or are we cursed?) with the gene that makes us set up LLCs, develop innovative products, launch websites, rent office space, court investors, and hire employees. We can hardly help ourselves. And hearing that another entrepreneur has done so successfully makes us salivate… at least, in the beginning it does. Success stories of other entrepreneurs can, later in life, invoke a tiny pang of regret, a sense of personal failure, a healthy measure of envy that we have not been able to achieve the same measure of triumph. We wonder if we are missing something — some knowledge, some charisma, some connection, some marketing strategy — that might have taken our business from the basement to the penthouse.

We know, intellectually, that businesses fail. In fact, the masses fail the majority of the time. And we also know, intellectually, that there are a thousand reasons why they fail: timing, financial resources, market conditions, world events, supply line issues, etc. Still, we can't help but look at ourselves and assume there is something about us that crashed the company's chances. And we are probably right. Most business analysts suggest that if a company is performing poorly, the first step is to fire the CEO. It makes sense, right? After all, the leadership of the company is as important to its longevity as the product, service, customer support, and customer engagement. If the CEO has allowed the business to tank, she must be replaced, presumably, with someone more knowledgeable, more experienced, and better equipped to take it where it needs to go.

The reality, however, is that almost no company has had such a Cinderella story and nearly hundred percent of entrepreneurs will tell you that their "instant success" has a dark and ominous backstory that would strike terror in the faint of heart. Their road to the top was anything but instant. It was long. It was hard. It was painful. Behind the multi-million dollar mansion, yachts, and magazine covers, the truth lurks as a stark reminder that starting a company is tough, and starting a successful one is significantly harder. Most fail at it the first few times. What is a person to do if they have tried and failed in business? If you've been bitten with the "business bug" like I have, there is no cure. You will never <u>not</u> want to be in business. Furthermore, there is only one treatment: start another business. There is nothing else we can do as serial entrepreneurs. Ideas come flying at us like bugs smacking against the windshield. Our friends and family grow tired of hearing us talk about one idea after another. Our families lose interest in the "next big thing" we sink our teeth into. And the people around us often start to see us as a little flaky and wonder if we really have what it takes to succeed. They watch us pour ourselves into what we are doing and fear that we are wasting away from the stress of it. They might even caution us to give it all up. When that happens, we may even lie to ourselves and promise to stop trying and get a "real job." But there is no "real job" for a business addict. When we get locked in on a mission, we are like a pitbull. Even when things go wrong, as they do with most businesses, we cry, dust ourselves off, and start again. So even though I had promised myself I would never venture into something like ScriptBook again even if given the second chance on a silver platter, running a company still meant a lot to me. The earlier I admitted this truth, the easier I could get through my grieving phase. As I have mentioned several times before, technology is the one thing that makes my toes tingle and gets me jumping out of bed in the morning, especially when it involves artificial intelligence.

I believe AI is ground-breaking, and if modelled and used properly, humanity could benefit a lot from it on a global scale. I have always held the opinion that science on its own sucks a great deal, and human beings left on their own suck as well. However, the combination of science and the human element could change the world in an unprecedented way. I believe the relationship between science and humanity cannot be overemphasized; even the unthinkable could be achieved with those two in a blissful romance. I don't know much about anything aside from science and technology. I don't know the first thing about cooking, cleaning, or entertaining. I guess I'm not conventional. All I care about is using technology for the betterment of the world. And that is why ScriptBook AI was so important to me. It signified something personal to me. Such was the nature of my grief. The blending of emotions sliced through me like a dagger sharpened by a whetstone. I was finally glad I could put ScriptBook behind me. But is it ever going to be really behind me? Probably not. The bitterness is gone. But I still feel the squeeze in my chest when I talk about it. I wish I had built something crappy. I wish it needed the revisions my counterparts at the dinner theater party talked about. If I had failed, it might have been easier to bear. But I built the best of the best.

CONCLUSION

Who am I without ScriptBook AI? It's a great question that will likely take me some years to fully answer. Check back with me in a few years. As I am rediscovering myself, a few things are certain. My optimism is returning as is my hopefulness. The wounds of ScriptBook's demise are fresh but healing. I doubt I will ever recover fully. After all, death is death and the grief it brings never truly ends. It only settles down from a scream into a whisper. But it is there, day and night, to remind you of what you lost. I often think of my brother… what his life might have been… how he might have walked through this with me. What ideas might he have offered? What encouragement might I have had from our conversations?

Death is a thief. It takes away the promise, but what dies doesn't disappear. It remains. ScriptBook AI, though dead and buried, is still somehow alive inside me. It always will be. And therein lies the source of the pain of mourning. It's a low hum that vibrates in the background of life all the time. ScriptBook was a major part of my life for seven years, and nothing can take that away from me. Neither can it be erased. However, now that I am free from it, I can never go back to it again even if I was given $50 million in venture capital. The injuries I endured left scars that still ache. I don't want to keep going down a self-destructive path. I am often asked, if I knew then what I know now, would I do it again? For me, it is a resounding no. If I knew I was going to suffer the way I suffered and lose what I lost, I would never have done it. If I knew I was going to pour my heart and soul into lines of code and present my masterpiece to the world only to be rejected, I would have spared myself the injury.

Go big or go home, they say. I went big. I went home too. The tarot cards have a card called the fool. The fool is depicted in the tarot as a happy go-lucky character. He has a bundle on a pole resting on his shoulders and he is joyfully setting off on an adventure. His smile is wide, toothy, and naive. That was me. The fool. Joyful. Naïve. Unaware. But the fool cannot remain so for long. The world will see to that. Reality ages you. When I reconnect with old friends who haven't seen me in the past few years, they wonder what happened. I can see it in the head tilt and the concerned gaze. I can hear it in the carefully worded questions. "Have you been sick?" Had I held on any longer, I would have been ready for the senior citizen's home! Even my mother noticed the way I had declined and the ever-widening bags under my eyes. She wondered what happened to her daughter, and I could sense she was worried about me. In fact, when I compared a picture from one of the interviews I had done on television just after raising capital, to how I looked the day of the bankruptcy filing, it seemed I aged twenty years. And I only ran ScriptBook for seven!

ScriptBook took a lot out of me. Correction! Hollywood did. No wonder actors and actresses keep their plastic surgeons on speed dial. The late-night worry sessions, pacing across the floor. The lies and backstabbing. The expectation of sycophancy. It's enough to make you vomit. Hollywood is a swamp bigger, muddier, and nastier than Washington D.C. And there are many more alligators in the Hollywood swamp waiting to snap you in two. At least politicians pretend to like you before they slaughter you.

Moving on from ScriptBook was a curse and a blessing. It was time to move on and writing this book provided the rebound I so desperately needed. There is no pressure this time as I write this story. There is no ticking time clock, no board, no investors, no bureaucrats. There is just the wonderful writing that keeps me tinkering day and night with something I have grown to love. To be fair, I wasn't that passionate about entertainment or Hollywood for that matter. I was never starstruck. Even meeting so many famous people, and walking around on legendary movie lots, my eyes remained fixed on my mission. My passion and ultimate, soul-reaching loyalty belonged to technology. Always has… always will. However, my quest to identify the gap within the movie industry, and to exploit that gap, cost me a lot of time, effort and energy in building a technological marvel for an industry that hardly deserves it.

The movie industry is a failing industry that is still clinging to its past glories. Within the industry, everything is crumbling and struggling, but on the outside, every part of it glimmers like gold. It lures in the unsuspecting and naïve like a hunter's trap. It promises something it can never deliver, but the sales pitch is nearly irresistible. Even those who "make" it in Hollywood admit that they are more prey than victor. They are only ever as good as their last success and the chase never ends. It's a diamond-encrusted hamster wheel where stars are afraid to gain a pound or a wrinkle and people behind the scenes scratch and claw for their next job. I didn't realize any of this when I started ScriptBook AI. But now that the company was gone, all I had was hindsight. This made me see the industry for what it truly is. Hollywood is not as great as people believe. I might consider myself lucky to have escaped it all. Perhaps this was the plan all along by powers higher than me. I don't know. But the loss of ScriptBook is not the end of the world anymore. I can breathe again. And I know my heart will go on and on. Sing it, Celine Dion!

With my emotional recovery well underway, I turned my attention to recapturing my physical wellness. Thankfully, I didn't need a plastic surgeon to come alive again. It's funny how the cure, sometimes, is to just stop consuming the poison. The dark circles disappeared. The sweet youthful glow resurfaced. I am back to being me — with the exception of that dull, faint, ache hiding in my heart. Even so, happiness is back. I have hope and faith in the future. We'll see what happens. But whatever happens, I am wiser and more ready to face it. For the first time in seven years, I am not holding my breath. I am free, and I know what I want to be when I grow up.

AUTHOR'S NOTE

I wrote The Chronicles Of A Female Tech Founder in February 2022, when the memories were still vivid and the loss of my company was an open wound. It took four years to finally bring the book into the world. During that time, I wrestled with deep doubt about whether I should tell this story at all, weighed down by the shame of failure. Eventually, I stopped letting doubt decide the fate of my story. I chose to self-publish this book—on my own terms.

There is one more thing I feel compelled to share.

When I founded ScriptBook, there was no AI hype. We were building data-driven models for film, not chasing buzzwords—still we were dismissed as snake oil. Today, the irony is hard to miss: "AI script analysis" is everywhere, but ScriptBook was delivering predictive analysis and box-office forecasts years before everyone else slapped GPT on a website and called it innovation.

Yet not all AI script tools are created equal.

Before the rise of large language models (GPT), companies like ScriptBook treated script analysis as a research problem. Our systems were built on years of machine-learning research, domain-specific datasets, and quantitative film analytics. Models were trained on structured metadata—box-office performance, genre patterns, character archetypes, narrative structure, sentiment arcs, dialogue density—signals proven to correlate with real-world outcomes. We published white papers, ran validation studies, and prioritized reproducibility. The outputs were not generative, but analytical—narrow in scope yet grounded in evidence.

The post-GPT era introduced a fundamentally different approach. Many modern script tools rely on large language models rather than bespoke film data or predictive modeling. They generate fluent summaries and stylistic feedback but without the research depth, domain-specific training, or long-term validation earlier systems required. What once took years to build and test can now be assembled in a fortnight.

There is also a cost to this shift. Large language models consume enormous amounts of energy and water at scale. As screenwriters, producers, and filmmakers adopt these tools, creative responsibility now extends beyond the page to the environmental footprint of the process itself.

Writers, producers, and filmmakers deserve clarity about what a script tool is actually doing. Summarizing scenes with confident-sounding word salad is not the same as evidence-based forecasts. One generates language. The other produces insight. One hallucinates. The other predicts.

In many ways, the evolution of AI script analysis mirrors Hollywood itself. Every genuine breakthrough risks becoming a sequel to its own hype. The challenge ahead is not to reject new tools, but to choose carefully—to value rigor over rhetoric, understanding over appearance.

My hope is that this conversation matures—that AI in storytelling becomes not louder, but wiser, and that "intelligence" is something these tools continue to earn, not merely claim.

ABOUT THE AUTHOR

N.D. Zerman is the founder of ScriptBook AI and DeepStory AI. Beyond her entrepreneurial endeavors, she has become a highly sought-after keynote speaker. Zerman's contributions have solidified her status as a thought leader in the intersection of AI and entertainment.

Her insights and innovative approaches have been featured in numerous media outlets, including CNN, The Times, Vogue Magazine, CNBC, Variety, The Guardian, and many others. She resides in Belgium, where she devotes her time to building mindful AI for the betterment of humanity.